"Dr. Pelè shows you just how much outbound marketing has changed, and helps you find your footing in a brand-new world of ideas." — **SETH GODIN**, author of THIS IS MARKETING

SOCIAL VELOCITY
WHY GOING FAST WON'T GET YOU FAR™

THE **3** PRINCIPLES OF CONSISTENT **CLIENT** ACQUISITION FOR HIGHLY-PAID EXPERTS

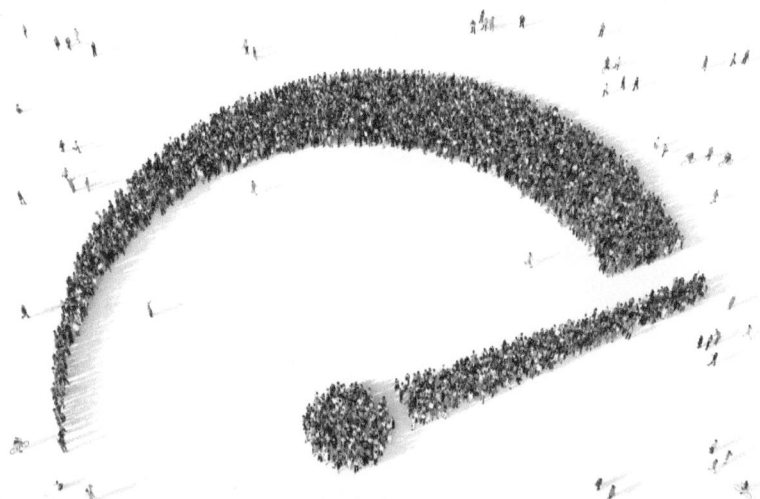

DR. PELÈ

Social Velocity

Copyright © 2021 Dr. Pelè

All rights reserved. No portion of this book may be reproduced, stored in a retrieval system, or transmitted in any form or by any means—electronic, mechanical, photocopy, recording, scanning, or other—without the prior written permission of the author.

The opinions and views offered in this book are in no way sponsored, affiliated, endorsed, authorized by, or associated with LinkedIn, Facebook, or YouTube.

ClientJam.com

For Rekiyatu: my wife, soul mate, best friend, and muse.
For my children: Ijeoma, Obinnamdi, and Ikennamefule.
For Profitable Happiness.

"Marketing is the new Production."
— *Dr. Pelè*

CONTENTS

Introduction VII

SECTION 1: THE MARKETING DILEMMA X
1. Why Most Marketing Fails 1
2. The Six Paradigm Shifts For Getting Known Online 19
3. The 3 Principles For Landing High-Value Clients 41

SECTION 2: GETTING SOCIAL VELOCITY 55
4. Principle One: RELATIONSHIPS 57
5. Why? 67
6. Who? 71
7. Where? 79
8. What? 83
9. How? 87
10. Principle Two: REACH 97
11. Strangers 109
12. Trust 117
13. Offer 125
14. Results 133
15. You 141
16. Principle Three: RESULTS 149
17. Conversions 159
18. Opportunities 163
19. Uniques 165
20. Numbers 169
21. Traffic 171

SECTION 3: LAUNCHING YOUR CLIENTJAM 175
22. Let's Talk About You 177
23. What Others Have Tried 181
24. Engagement Radio 185
25. White-Hat C.E.O. 191
26. ClientJam 199

Introduction

You've earned your stripes. You've paid your dues. You are highly credible in your business niche and you have the past customer success and credentials to prove it. But when it comes to social media, something seems to be holding you back from successfully marketing to and attracting your best clients like you once did. And the result is so debilitating that your business now seems to have a questionable future.

Yet this 'something' holding you back is invisible to you. It's difficult to see for two reasons:

1) It is a behavioral habit.
2) It is *your* behavioral habit.

This book is about how to break the behavioral habits getting in the way of success for so many entrepreneurs and companies in today's social landscape. This book is also about how to install a new way of thinking, a shift in paradigm from an old way of doing business to a new way that will work regardless of the technology or business landscape of the day.

In these pages, you will see how a simple shift from *speed* to *velocity* can make all the difference in your business. We will explore the three principles of *Social Velocity*, each with a five-part framework that will change not only how your marketing works but also how you deliver value to your clients.

Through teaching, writing, and building our software and community at ClientJam™, we have helped hundreds of consultants, coaches, companies, and creative entrepreneurs worldwide make the shift from speed to Social Velocity. While much of our focus will be on *LinkedIn*, the principles explained here will apply to *Facebook*, *YouTube*, or any social network whatsoever. The proven ideas and tested systems presented in this book will therefore work for you regardless of industry, niche, or social network, because they are based on the constants of human psychology and behavior.

To get the best out of this book, I suggest you do the following:

1. Understand and internalize the 3 principles and 15 frameworks of Social Velocity.
2. Answer the questions at the end of each chapter in Section Two, so you can develop your Social Velocity marketing strategy.
3. Create a free account on ClientJam.com, where you can launch and measure your Social Velocity marketing strategy for landing high-value clients on LinkedIn, Facebook, YouTube, or other social media outlets.

Marketing has changed because technology has evolved, and the world has changed. It is time to put an end to the business behaviors that keep us running with great speed on a hamster wheel, going nowhere. Companies, business leaders, and entrepreneurs that continue to depend on behaviors they think will help them go *fast* will miss out on the rich rewards of going *far*. It is time to shift our paradigm from speed to velocity.

Ready? Set? Let's go!

Dr. Pelè

SECTION 1:
THE MARKETING DILEMMA

Dr. Pelè

1. Why Most Marketing Fails

Is Marketing dead? Or did it merely leave the building? Either way, something is wrong. Customers no longer depend heavily on your content to learn about a solution to their problem. If they have a problem, they can just 'Google' it. If you're a service-based business owner, no one seems to care about your service—no matter how good it may be—unless they have a *relationship* with you. And why should they? In a world of almost infinite choices, the winner is sometimes simply the one who showed up.

In today's deafening, technology-enabled noise we call social media, where everyone has all the tools they could ever need to contribute generously to the cacophony, how on Earth do you stand out above the crowd? How do you get seen and heard by your ideal prospects so you can get a shot at eventually turning them into clients?

This book is about the reality that you can't blindly follow the status quo (what most people seem to be doing on social media) and expect positive results in today's new and evolving business landscape.

But this book is also about hope.

Consultants, companies, experts, and entrepreneurs everywhere are looking for ways to break through the noise and position themselves as authorities in their niches. The good news is that success is possible if one is willing to adopt a new way to think about marketing. One must accept that marketing as we once knew it is dead, or at best, in dire need of a reincarnation.

So, let's start with a currently accepted definition of marketing, according to the American Marketing Association (AMA)[1]:

"Marketing is the activity, set of institutions, and processes for creating, communicating, delivering, and exchanging offerings that have value for customers, clients, partners, and society at large." (Approved 2017).

The key word here is 'offerings', which is too easily misinterpreted by far too many to mean 'products and services'. This definition may have once been fine, but in today's jaded, hyper-crowded business environment, the mere suggestion of a product or service, or exchange of offerings—or anything having to do with sales—will send people running for shelter.

This definition of marketing is no longer sustainable for the business leader or entrepreneur trying to stand out in a social media crowd where so many people seem to think it's okay to throw their sales pitches into your email inbox and yell about their services everywhere you turn.

This definition of marketing is—unfortunately—the status quo, and it is destroying people's businesses.

In today's world, successful marketing is more than an exchange of offerings. It must be about building *relationships* if it is to be effective.

If you want to sell something, you can't be perceived as overtly selling! Ironically, the kind of marketing that works best in today's crowded world is something that doesn't feel or look like marketing at all. It has to be spaced out over time, grown organically, and feel only indirectly related to a product or service.

Yes, it's easy to blame everything on marketing. But what if what we're seeing isn't a marketing problem? What if the real problem is today's rapid advancement of technology? What if the real issue is that technology has become such a powerful enabler of things that it has exposed and expanded some undesirable aspects of our human nature?

THE NEED FOR SPEED

I remember once gifting a 1-1 mentorship meeting over Zoom to a member of my online LinkedIn community. Let's call him 'David' for convenience. I had promised him an hour—with no strings attached—so he could get some feedback from me about how his marketing was working (or not). For most of our time together, he was in tears because of some extreme feelings of hopelessness he was experiencing.

"Dr. Pelè," he said, making direct eye-contact with me through his webcam. "I just don't know how to get clients as quickly and reliably as I once did."

He paused to wipe his eyes.

"Before the pandemic, I could give a speech somewhere, or send an email to my mailing list and sell my coaching courses in a matter of hours. Now, there's no traffic in my funnels and I'm one hundred percent at the mercy of referrals. It seems like I have no marketing strategy at all. I don't even know how I will pay my bills next month."

He heaved forward and covered his eyes, apologizing for crying so much. "I just really don't know what to do next."

I allowed him some time to let the crying subside. When he had regained his composure, I started sharing my perspective, carefully, so as not to unintentionally trigger another fit of tears.

"David, I agree with you," I said. "You have technology and funnels, but no functioning marketing strategy. The good news is, that's not necessarily a bad thing. That simply means you can start afresh and do it right this time."

His eyes brightened with what I thought was a glimmer of hope.

"You just need to do things differently," I continued. "What we used to call marketing is not very effective anymore. The world moved from *interruption* marketing to *permission* marketing, but with the proliferation of technology and content creation tools, we now live in a world of instant gratification, noise, and overwhelm where even the best-intentioned permission marketing doesn't work as well as it used to. We need a new kind of marketing."

"Got it," he said, cocking his head and rolling his eyes as if to remind me that this was no time for my doctoral theories. "But what can I do right *now* for getting clients quickly and reliably?"

"I can help you with the 'reliability' part," I said, "But I want you to stop thinking so much about *speed*."

From the look of shock that immediately grew on his face, I think he must have concluded I hadn't been listening. He had bills to pay right now and a speedy solution was the entire point of our conversation.

Which part of *now* didn't I understand?

HOW SPEED CAN DESTROY YOUR BUSINESS

Later that same week, I was blessed with the honor and opportunity to interview the incomparable Seth Godin on The

Profitable Happiness™ Podcast; my weekly show where I highlight the stories and wisdom of highly successful experts, thought leaders, and entrepreneurs. If you've been living under a rock for the past decade (or two) and haven't heard of Seth Godin, then you have missed out on someone and something truly special. Seth is none other than the father of 'permission marketing', the inventor of 'email marketing', and frankly, one of this generation's greatest business thinkers. He is the author of over 20 books and counting and has been inducted into the American Marketing Association's Hall of Fame.

Speaking for the first time with my all-time marketing mentor over zoom that day, I was lost in a sea of questions I desperately wanted to ask in the short time we had together. Our main topic was his latest book at the time—*The Practice*—which focuses on the need for business professionals and creatives of any kind to learn to stop obsessing about outcomes and develop the habit of consistently 'shipping' their works of creativity. But I wanted to start by asking him about marketing. I wanted to ask him how marketing has evolved ever since he invented permission marketing. I wanted to ask him about the role of technology in today's world, and how to get heard above the noise on social media. My mind raced throughout the interview until I was finally able to find a relevant spot to ask him for his current definition of marketing. Here's what he said:

*"Marketing is not advertising, or hype, or spam. Marketing is making things better by making better things. Marketing is the true story we tell about what we do that gets other people to talk about it, that changes something. If you're not trying to change something, if you don't stand for something, then it's not going to work, and you're not a marketer. You're just **hustling**."*
— Seth Godin *on the Profitable Happiness™ Podcast*[2]

I remember responding enthusiastically, "Wow, that would make a lot of people **hustlers** today who think they are marketers!" This exchange perfectly captured for me the sentiment that is destroying so many potentially great businesses before they even get a chance to start. It also reminded me instantly of my conversation with David. Instead of *giving* value, he was focused on *taking*, and doing so with speed. Sadly, I realized that I would have to consider what he was doing merely hustling, not marketing.

So many engage in marketing that has devolved into this desperate, pervasive 'hustling', powered by browser-based bots, automation, and a need for instant business gratification.

How many times have you opened your email just to discover someone you don't know asking you to pay them thousands of dollars for a course you care nothing about? And how many times have you logged onto social media to see automated direct messages from random strangers inviting you to a meeting about a problem they say you have (after somehow magically diagnosing it without your participation)?

All of these behaviors have become so widely adopted that 'hustling' for instant results has become the status quo on social media. The result? When so many people behave this way, marketing gets a bad name. Businesses struggle to get seen and heard through the noise. Over time, clients get jaded, tune you out, and you lose money.

Following my learning from Seth Godin, I henceforth used the term 'hustling' to describe behaviors that are inspired by a desire to get to the sale quickly. Hustling is when you want to go from 'click to customer' in one meeting. It's when you want to go from introduction to contract in 24 hours. And it's when you find yourself offering to solve people's problems before carefully listening to learn if they have a problem in the first place.

This is not marketing. It's a bad version of speed dating on steroids, and if you get involved in these behaviors they can damage the reputation of your business. Over time, they could destroy your business entirely.

THE PROBLEM WITH HUSTLING

Today's social media is overrun with a myth of instant success, and our collective addiction to smartphones and computer technology has only exacerbated this problem. What many don't realize is that when we are overly indulgent in instant gratification and hustling, we are rewiring our brains to endanger our future financial, social, and health outcomes.

There is a parallel definition around hustling in the world of work. For many people, it refers to a culture of constant, hard work. For some, there is even a sense of pride attached to being known or seen as a hustler. And for others, there is a growing backlash against this 'hustle culture' phenomenon because of its potential to be more harmful than helpful.

When you combine hustle culture and the desire for instant, speedy marketing outcomes, you get a truly destructive mix. For this conversation, the kind of hustling we're talking about is a set of behaviors associated with a relentless desire for speedy outcomes, especially as it happens within a marketing and sales context.

Given this context, in case you're thinking that 'hustling' does not apply to you, here are a few pervasive behaviors that amount to the same thing:

Lack of Personalization

Whenever you send mass messages by email or direct message (DM) on social media that have absolutely no personalization in them, you're being driven by speed and a desire for mass results. Think of the recipients. How will they receive your message? Sadly, most people who send these messages don't think carefully about how *each* person on the other end of their message will feel. This is the best way to get your messages ending up in the trash and it is a clear example of hustling.

Random Connection Requests

When you send connection requests to people you don't know, they may accept the request based on a review of your profile. However, it's what you do next that can build or destroy the relationship before it starts. Don't immediately start vomiting the value of your offerings and inviting them to a 1-1 meeting to solve their problems. Let the relationship evolve more naturally. Think about it. If you met someone you didn't know on the street somewhere, would you immediately ask them to join you in your car for a conversation about their business? Probably not. So why ask for such a huge initial commitment from a total stranger? This also is an example of hustling.

Solution Upsells

Even if you're not guilty of spamming people in the business development process, are you aware of how your solution delivery is perceived by your customers? I once paid $10,000 for a course, only to get thrown into a vault of videos. No one was ever available to provide any 1-1 attention to my issues and every time I asked for help, they tried to upsell me into their $30,000 program. Seriously? What has become of the idea that we should be 'delivering value' to our clients? Nowadays, too many online solutions providers are trying to hustle clients into the next more expensive program in their solution 'value ladders'.

Not good.

So, why is this all happening in the first place? What is it about our human nature that so quickly devolves into this kind of hustling? Why is marketing being destroyed by instant gratification? And most importantly, what is the cure?

YOUR BRAIN ON MARSHMALLOWS

For answers, we can turn to a seminal experiment that was conducted at Stanford University in the 1960s by Walter Mischel[3], a renowned Austrian-born American psychologist who specialized in social psychology. This experiment added scientific validity and insight into what is already recognized throughout humankind's history as perhaps one of the most important attributes of success in life and business: *delayed gratification*.

In this study, Dr. Mischel placed preschool children alone in a room and offered them marshmallows with two conditions, either instant gratification or delayed gratification. On the one hand, each child was told that if they did not eat the marshmallow placed in front of them for the ten minutes they were left alone, they would receive a reward of two marshmallows later. And on the other hand, they were told that if they went ahead and ate the marshmallow before the time was up, they would not get a second one.

So, this was the choice. Hustle for an instant reward now, or delay gratification and get increased rewards later.

After the ten minutes were up and the researchers returned, there was a clear distribution of behavior. Some children had eaten the one marshmallow in front of them and others had exercised the patience to wait for the greater reward they all knew would come later. But this was not where the truly shocking result of this study was seen.

Over more than 40 years later, researchers followed up on the progress of these children and discovered that those who were able to delay gratification ended up with greater success outcomes in life, such as higher academic achievement and other physiological measures associated with self-control.

This evidence was certainly powerful, except for the fact that it did not rule out any inherent traits or trust biases of the children involved. There was still an open question of whether or not delayed gratification was something anyone could learn and nurture, regardless of inherent traits and biases.

For this, a second set of experiments later showed that delayed gratification is something that can be learned and its important benefits are available to us all. Researchers at the University of Rochester[4] decided to revisit the Marshmallow experiments, but this time, they created two environments with different levels of trust. One environment involved unreliable outcomes and low trust. For example, the researcher would promise a positive outcome (like a box of crayons), but never delivered on the promise. The second environment provided high trust and more reliable outcomes (the researchers kept their promises and delivered the box of crayons).

The result was that over time, the children in the group with clarity of trusted outcomes were able to train their brains to delay gratification, while the group with lower trust and lack of reliable outcomes gave in to the desire for instant gratification.

What these experiments made clear is that if we can develop a sense of clarity and certainty about the outcomes we hope for, we are more able to delay gratification to achieve them in the long run.

This may sound simple, but unfortunately, it isn't. In the human mind, there is a constant battle between the limbic, emotional brain, and the neocortex, logical brain. The emotional brain wants instant gratification and dopamine *now*, while the logical brain can focus on the long term and direct a person's energies appropriately.

So, which brain will win? If we want to grow our businesses through social media interactions, we will have to learn to empower our logical brains before our emotional brains take over. But how do we achieve this? How do we make the shift from the natural tendency for *speedy*, instant gratification that is getting in the way of our business success?

THE PARABLE OF THE HAMSTER WHEEL

Picture this. You are a hamster and your owner has just invited you to step on a hamster wheel. With a smile, he encourages you to get in and go as fast as you possibly can. You oblige him.

You get on, and you start running. You go fast, gaining incredible speed. At first, the adrenaline rush is exhilarating. Soon, you get tired and as you observe the glee in your highly entertained owner's face, you ask yourself for the first time, "why exactly am I doing this? Why am I obsessed with going fast, but getting nowhere? How can I shift from merely going fast to also going far?"

When you ask these questions, you are finally ready to step off the hamster wheel of business hustling and adopt a different, longer-term paradigm of success. You are ready to say goodbye to hustling that gets you nowhere. You are ready to develop certainty about a delayed outcome, which will help you slow down. As they say, 'slow and steady wins the race', right?

But what metaphor will you adopt to build confidence in a delayed, future result? With all the shiny objects buzzing past us every day on social media, how can we replace speed as our driving paradigm?

This question was answered for me when I considered the relationship between speed and *velocity*.

If you remember from high school physics, speed is a scalar quantity that describes going fast, but it doesn't necessarily have to involve a *direction*. This means you could be going fast, but also going nowhere, such as on a treadmill or a hamster wheel. On the other hand, velocity is the vector quantity of going fast, but in a specified *direction*.

Speed = how *fast* you move
(eg. 60 mph, but potentially going nowhere)

Velocity = how *far* you move
(eg. 60mph, going in a specific direction, such as north)

The difference between speed and velocity—when used as a business metaphor—is useful because it can help us produce behavior changes that translate into more ethical, productive marketing. Velocity takes its place as a superior metaphor because it tells you more than how fast you're going; it also tells you *where* you're going. If your focus is exclusively on speed, and you don't know the direction in which your speed is taking you, then you could easily be headed toward harmful outcomes for your business.

FROM SPEED TO VELOCITY ON LINKEDIN

To make the shift from speed to velocity on LinkedIn, we have to first step off the hamster wheel and stop hustling strangers to turn them into *connections*. Next, we need to adopt new strategies that attract LinkedIn or Facebook *followers* and encourage them to voluntarily MOVE in our direction.

The core strategy you use to create these shifts on social media is by sharing HELPFUL content.

On social media sites like LinkedIn and Facebook, there is a rush by many to CONNECT with people and immediately start selling to them. This is hustling and it doesn't work. What works instead, is to become a thought leader and begin to attract FOLLOWERS. When you connect with people on LinkedIn, their motivation to accept may have nothing to do with you (a lot of people say yes merely to grow the size of their connections). Whereas, when people follow you, it is a voluntary action taken because they genuinely want to learn more from you.

SPEED	VELOCITY
Sending COLD connection requests to people based on title or keywords	Posting HELPFUL content to the feed to attract voluntary Followers
Direct messaging random people with your offer	Occasionally using calls-to-action in your content to introduce your offer
Spammy, seller-focused content; no help or value delivered	Voluntary, buyer-focused, helpful, valuable content
You're seen as just another Hustler	You're seen as a thought leader

There is a saying that if you think you're a leader and you look behind and no one is following, you're not a leader: you're merely taking a walk. The same goes for *thought* leadership. So many of us would like to be seen as thought leaders, but to truly become one, you have to be in the business of attracting followers.

When you shift from *only* seeking to grow connections on LinkedIn to a focus on growing followers, your social media behavior will completely change and so will the quality of your results. You will soon realize that being HELPFUL and providing valuable content is the number one thing you can do to grow your business through social media.

IT'S TIME FOR A PARADIGM SHIFT

Social Velocity is the quality of sharing *helpful* content so that your ideal clients voluntarily *move* toward you. The result of Social Velocity is that more of your ideal clients will discover you, like you, and trust you enough to eventually BUY something from you. Social Velocity is what happens when you rethink traditional marketing and focus on helpful, consistent *content* marketing. And finally, Social Velocity is what delivers on the promise of clients coming to you—inbound—without you having to advertise or go seek them out.

However, achieving Social Velocity will require a clear and intentional paradigm shift away from certain current ways of doing things online.

You've probably heard of the concept of shifting paradigms and if so, you'll know that it's a significant effort that produces a completely different way of looking at things in both life and business. (For example, most people once thought the Earth was flat. Changing beliefs to the idea of a round Earth was a significant paradigm shift.)

One of the most well-known ideas demonstrating how paradigm shifts work was presented by Thomas Kuhn[5], the American philosopher who pioneered the concept. He used the visual illusion below.

What do you see when you look at this image? Do you see a duck or a rabbit? Or both?

Kuhn used this illusion to demonstrate the idea that a paradigm shift occurs when you can look at the same information but perceive and understand it in an entirely different way.

This is what we have to do to 'uninstall' some of the behaviors we have become accustomed to on social media and instead, adopt new behaviors that will help us grow our businesses more reliably in the long term.

If you're ready to grow your business predictably and steadily, then keep reading. If you're ready to adopt a mindset of sharing helpful content consistently to grow your thought leadership on social media, then keep reading. And if you're ready to embrace some significant new ways of looking at your business, then read on.

It's time to make the shift from 'speed' to 'velocity'.

2. The Six Paradigm Shifts For Getting Known Online

Follow me as a young child into the jungles behind our war-torn African village; from one refugee camp that was no longer as safe as we once thought, to a new one we'd just heard about where there were fewer bombs, less fighting, and a greater chance for survival. This was my life as an Igbo, a Biafran fugitive during the Nigerian Civil War of the late 1960s. My mother and I, along with others from our village, were experiencing what was called *Osondu*—the race for life—as we existed nomadically in the bushes, trying desperately to stay alive.

It was in that jungle, in that time of fear and hunger, that I learned two great life lessons that have stayed with me until today, here in the safety and sanctuary of America, my adopted country. The first was the lesson of *happiness*. And the second was the lesson of *content*.

As the Nigerian side's bombs were whizzing by overhead and hunger ravaged us, my mother did the strangest thing. Holding me in her arms, neither able to give me food nor save me from the bombs, she did the next best thing she could at the time.

She sang to me.

She would invent stories and sing them to me as songs of food, safety, and dreams of traveling far away from that place of danger, inserting my name in every verse.

And her songs made me happy.

In that moment, I learned that *happiness* is so powerful that it can drive away fear and hunger. I also discovered music and story, my lifelong friends, who have been my faithful companions ever since. But most importantly, I learned that happiness comes before success and not the other way around. This is why today I am a musician, author, and storyteller on The Profitable Happiness™ Podcast. Happiness leaves clues.

In that defining moment, I learned the second most important lesson of my life. I learned that *content* is a powerful strategy for survival.

You see, what my mother did in that moment was use content to divert my attention from the pain and fear of dying. To mitigate those concerns, she used music and story to *transport* my thoughts to a place where my spirit came alive. I was engaged and the fear all around us was rendered invisible.

Much as one might give young children puzzles and games to occupy their time during a long road trip so they don't obsessively ask, "are we there yet?" my mother's songs focused my attention on love and hope.

Little did I know in those childhood experiences that years later, I would be researching for my Ph.D. on the transportational power of narrative and *storytelling* as an entrepreneurial best practice.

Here's a quote from that 2007 graduate thesis:

"Business storytelling is a conduit for communicating entrepreneurial leadership vision, navigating organizational change, and achieving influence with partners,

suppliers, and prospective clients. The ability to influence and persuade prospects and stakeholders through the process of business narrative is critical to a firm's ability to grow and succeed." - Dr. Pelè [6]

Had I known what I know now, I could have skipped the hundred-thousand-dollar student loan and just asked my mother—and every other parent with restless kids on a road trip—about the power of content!

My graduate thesis, experiments, and research showed me that perhaps the most powerful four-word phrase in the world is, "once upon a time…" When we hear it, we relax. The same transportational effect comes from music and other forms of content. Our brains become willing receptors, anxious and happy to follow the storyteller or singer to the magical land she is about to describe. A place of infinite promise, of dreams, and meaning.

This is the secret of great *content* marketing: the ability to divert the attention of your audience from the natural fear of being sold to, and instead, transport them to a place where they feel rooted and present in a topic of interest. It is a secret rooted in the age-old power of storytelling—whether through words, music, or learning—to psychologically move us to a different place where *trust* can be safely built.

Adopting a content marketing mindset is the first paradigm shift we need to transform our business development approach from speed to velocity.

Indeed, I like to say that *content creates clients*! If we want to leverage the relationship-building power of content, we have to first choose to slow down and get off the hustling hamster wheel. Through our content, we are then able to create Social Velocity, an environment that feels safe enough to our intended audience so they can begin to voluntarily *move* in our direction.

A BRIEF HISTORY OF CONTENT MARKETING

Content marketing is the act of using interesting content to build awareness and trust, and it does so *indirectly* as you pull people closer to your brand. It has seen incredible and steady growth in public interest, especially through social media since around 2010, as can be seen below from Google Trends[7]:

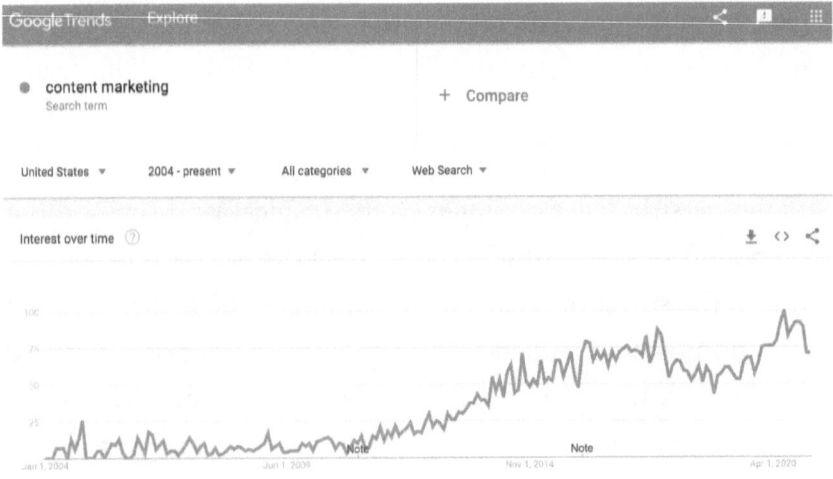

So, who is a content marketer? One could argue that anyone with an intended outcome who uses indirect teaching or storytelling to pull people in is a content marketer. That very broad definition might make even Jesus Christ a content marketer, given his use of parables and healing activities to grow trust among his audience. It would certainly make my mother a content marketer to me, her audience of one. But the one content marketer—in a business context—that I have found most fascinating is Benjamin Franklin, who has the distinction of being perhaps the earliest recorded 'intentional' content marketer in history.

In 1732, Benjamin Franklin published his first almanac under the pen name Richard Saunders[8]. This almanac—titled *Poor Richard's Almanack*—was credited with being a hidden reason behind what would eventually be his most successful business venture; becoming the official printer of Pennsylvania, New Jersey, and Delaware.

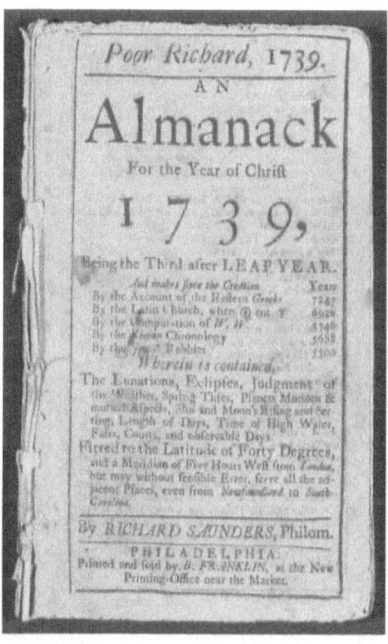

For 25 years, he indirectly promoted his printing business through the excellent, entertaining, and valuable content that he provided in his almanac. It was also in every way a commercial success on its merit, selling as many as 10,000 copies per year. But what I found most interesting was the way Benjamin Franklin himself described the primary intention behind it:

"In 1732 I first published my Almanack under the name of Richard Saunders; it was continued by me about twenty-five years, and commonly called Poor Richard's Almanack. I endeavored to make it both entertaining and useful, and it accordingly came to be in such demand, that I reaped considerable profit from it, vending annually near ten thousand." - Benjamin Franklin[9]

The key phrase here is his intention to make it "both entertaining and useful," which created the high demand that led to his eventual business success. The other important point is his use of the pseudonym, Richard Saunders; a clear attempt at diverting attention from himself, thereby creating a safe space for his audience to focus on the content, not his business offers.

This is the power and core strategy of content marketing. He didn't focus his content on selling or advertising his printing business. That would surely have driven his audience away. He didn't even talk about printing in the publication at all. Beyond the printing credit given to his "New Printing Office near the Market," there was no mention of his name or his business. And yet, this 'side' publication became one of the most powerful reasons for his success as a printer.

Just as my mother focused my attention on things that would interest me, Benjamin Franklin gave recurring value to his audience, which in turn built the trust that led to his business success.

The mistake I find so many professionals making online is the eagerness to only share information that is directly related to their businesses. We promote our services and demonstrate expertise, but we fail to realize that the most powerful and overarching strategy is to merely keep the *attention* of our audience. And doing so does not always have to involve promoting your business directly. The more indirect a majority of our content is, the better.

Take a look at the history of content marketing, of which Benjamin Franklin was merely a great first example. Ever since, businesses the world over have figured out and implemented the power of content marketing. Here are a few notable examples of great—and indirect—content marketing strategies over time:

1. 1732: Benjamin Franklin published his *Poor Richard's Almanac* to indirectly promote his printing business.
2. 1895: John Deere published *The Furrow*, a print magazine designed for farmers
3. 1900: Michelin published the *Michelin Guide* with guidance about auto maintenance and travel
4. 1933: Procter & Gamble invented the 'soap opera' genre by using a series of interesting stories on a radio program to indirectly market their soap products.
5. 1987: Lego launched *Brick Kicks* magazine featuring games, comics and modeling tips, and interesting information based on their toy.
6. 2006: Blendtec shares its 'Will it Blend?' series of videos on YouTube, receiving over 235 million views.
7. 2014: *The Lego Movie* is arguably the first (highly successful) feature-length movie credited with being a content marketing effort.

What we can learn from these great examples is the power of indirect content to gain attention, engage, and grow the interest of ideal clients.

Admittedly, most of the examples we've looked at so far were well-funded campaigns by major business concerns. Can the solo entrepreneur or small business similarly leverage the power of content marketing?

Simply put—and enthusiastically stated—YES!

With the proliferation of online technology, smartphones, and a global audience, anyone who is willing to slow down, get off the hustling hamster wheel and adopt Social Velocity can be a content marketer. The only remaining question is how to become an *effective* one.

EFFECTIVE CONTENT MARKETING

In our software and community of practice at ClientJam, we teach three core principles to help our clients leverage Social Velocity and content marketing to attract high-value clients on LinkedIn (and other platforms). We call it the 3Rs, *Relationships*, *Reach*, and *Results*. Within each of the 3Rs, we have different five-part frameworks that deliver the promise of each parent principle. Our clients use this model and system to launch end-to-end psychology and technology business funnels that bring them clients through the magnetic power of content marketing and analytics. Here is our definition of content marketing that guides the 3Rs:

"Content Marketing is the use of content to build RELATIONSHIPS, extend the REACH of your brand, and increase business RESULTS as more of your ideal clients become aware of you, trust you, and buy from you over time." — Dr. Pelè

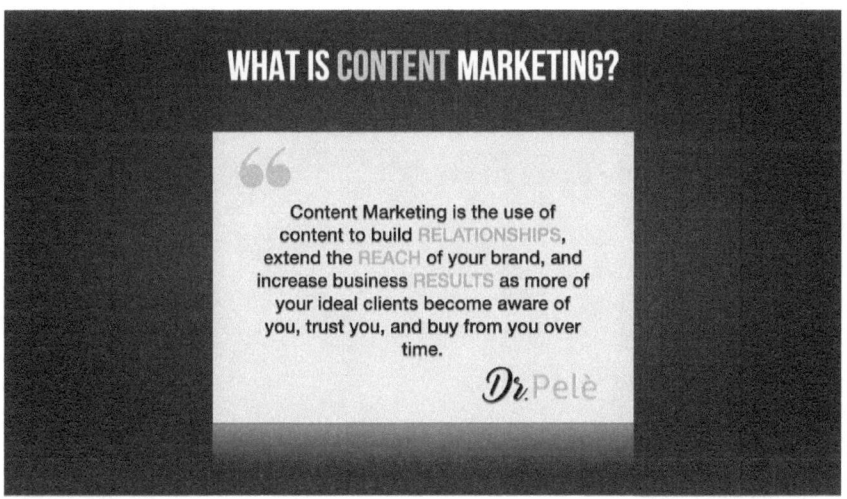

We will cover the 3Rs of Social Velocity in greater detail in the next chapter. First, let's discuss the five remaining paradigm shifts we need to prepare ourselves for *effective* content marketing.

1. Focus Over Overwhelm
2. Buyer Over Seller
3. Followers Over Connections
4. Service Over Selling
5. Fact Over Fiction

FOCUS OVER OVERWHELM

Most people are just too busy. To some degree, being busy has almost become a kind of comfort zone, providing a feeling of false safety in a crowded world of massive uncertainty. There is so much noise on social media that I would dare say successfully standing out from the crowd is perhaps one of the most impressive things one can do in today's business landscape.

As a result of all the noise, far too many of us suffer from technology, information, and social media overwhelm. We are literally drowning in *hustle*! Take a look at some of the things we find ourselves doing every single day:

- Sharing on Facebook
- Building Marketing Funnels
- Posting on LinkedIn
- Updating Twitter and Instagram
- Uploading videos to YouTube
- Writing Blog Posts
- Buying Courses
- Joining Masterminds
- Teaching for Free
- Delivering Workshops
- And more … all without a clear plan!

Sometimes, one wants to just give up! It's no wonder people need to 'unplug' sometimes just to maintain some sanity.

And yet, with all the shiny objects around us, we know intuitively that nothing works unless we are focused. But don't take it from me. Three of the world's greatest business leaders were all asked what their number one secret to success was. To a person, Bill Gates, Warren Buffet, and Steve Jobs all answered with one word: *Focus*.

They all believed that focus was the foundation of their success. Indeed, your business is like a house. If the foundation is weak, the facades will crumble. You don't need all the shiny objects, complicated funnels, up-sells and down-sells, blogging, a massive online audience, expensive tools, or to be 'internet-famous'. All you need is a focus on:

- ONE content marketing plan
- ONE social network
- ONE ideal client avatar

We will be going into detail about these when we discuss the RELATIONSHIPS principle in the next chapter. In that section, we will discuss how to create and document your ONE content marketing plan that will deliver results. We will also propose that, for most business owners and entrepreneurs, the ONE social network where you can build relationships is *LinkedIn*. Finally, we will go into detail about how to create and document your ONE, ideal, high-value, client avatar.

At the end of the day, your goal is to be visible and helpful to the select group of people on a social platform who are your ideal clients. Focusing on this—through a clear plan of action—will prepare you for overall content marketing success.

BUYER OVER SELLER

One of my favorite business constructs is what I call, 'The Buyer To Seller Continuum'. Imagine a continuum where on the one hand you have communication strategies that are all about you, the seller. Then imagine on the other end of that continuum, communication strategies that are all about your buyer. The space between these two extremes is The Buyer To Seller Continuum. What you want to do is examine every single post, email, message, web page, or content you produce on social media and simply ask yourself, "who am I talking about here? Myself, or my buyer?"

Most of our newer ClientJam clients who try this simple exercise are surprised to discover that in almost everything they've put out, whether it is their profile or their posts, they have been talking about *themselves*, not their customers. In a world of shiny objects and short attention spans, if you're not talking about your customer, no one will stop to listen to what you're saying.

Here's a short excerpt from how I described this challenge in one of my earlier books: *Big-Ticket Clients*:

> *"Far too many online marketers are in the business of becoming famous, as opposed to being in the business of helping people. These marketers show up talking about themselves—the sellers—and how much money they've made in their coaching and consulting businesses. Their entire marketing approach is seller-focused. They alone are the hero of the story they are telling, and the buyer is frankly just one of the trophies they acquire along the way."* — Dr. Pelè, *Big-Ticket Clients*[10]

THE BUYER-TO-SELLER CONTINUUM

We have to clarify and simplify our marketing content, but most of all, we have to step into the minds of the people in our intended audience, complete their sentences, answer their questions, and talk about *them*. If we don't address this fundamental aspect of human nature—our clients' needs to feel that they are the hero of the story we're telling—we will not be heard or seen, no matter how much content we publish online.

In the coming sections about the REACH principle, we will introduce strategies that help us focus our communications on our buyers and do so in a way that is interesting, entertaining, and educational.

FOLLOWERS OVER CONNECTIONS

One of the simplest and most important shifts I have made in growing my influence on LinkedIn is to reduce sending out invitations for people to *connect* with me, and instead, focus on attracting people to *follow* my content. The implicit requirement of this shift is that you must now truly become a thought leader.

If you think about Facebook, their social paradigm is built around the idea of connecting with 'friends' to gain access to their content over time. Besides the dubious fact that most of the so-called friends you connect with aren't friends in the true sense of the word, the relationship one maintains with most of those connections is at best, shallow.

On the other hand, if you think about Twitter or YouTube, the social paradigm on both networks is exclusively followership. As of this writing there is no way to 'connect' on those platforms. Instead, people can follow each other's content over time.

One unique aspect of LinkedIn's social paradigm is that it features both the ability to connect with people (and simultaneously follow them), or merely follow them alone. What usually happens is that most people default to connecting with as many people as they can as a strategy to expand their network.

When you compare the two strategies—connections versus followers—you'll see that they inspire and produce different behaviors:

Connections:

- Quantity and *speed* of connections do not equate to quality and depth of relationships because most people accept and invite connections purely to *quickly* grow what they believe is a larger network. Going fast won't get you far. This is the core difference between speed and velocity.
- Connections are the prime focus of interruption-marketing 'hustlers' because they believe that the free direct message they can send you might just have you clicking on their instant sales offer. (This spammy behavior may have worked at one time, but not so much anymore).
- LinkedIn's algorithm doesn't appear to send your content to a large number of 1st-degree connections as much as it once may have. Many have confirmed through their testing that organic reach on LinkedIn (and other networks) has significantly reduced.
- You can connect *fast* with many people and get nowhere in your business relationships with them.

Followers:

- When people follow you willingly because your content spoke to them, a voluntary relationship is created, which has much greater *velocity* and potential for future business success built in.

- When you focus on attracting followers, you essentially become a thought leader. This is the core strategy behind being an authority that people are drawn to, versus you having to always *push* out information that interrupts people.
- Followers involve a larger natural audience on LinkedIn beyond your 1st-degree direct connections. When you focus on this strategy, your posted content can organically reach 2nd- and 3rd-degree users, thereby significantly expanding your reach.
- Earning voluntary followers will take you *far* in terms of the potential to build beneficial business relationships with them over time.

The strategy of connecting on LinkedIn has been abused and overrun with automation and bots, all of which violate LinkedIn's terms of service (TOS). An entire industry of software companies offering quick and easy ways of auto-connecting with people and then immediately selling them things has seriously undermined LinkedIn's goal of being a place where genuine business relationships are built. As a result, they have seriously clamped down on automation tools and have put limitations on the number of connections one can make. Consider the following message that many have received:

You've reached the invitation limit

For a quality network, we recommend connecting with people you know. For others, you can follow to see their posts or message.

Learn more   Got it

This message from LinkedIn says it all. When you gain followers because they engage with your content, it becomes easier—and more appropriate—to connect with them and continue a direct messaging conversation.

Not only do you avoid violating LinkedIn's rules, but you really do make yourself much more attractive to potential clients when you reorient your profile, content, and business development strategy toward first gaining followers, and then connections over time.

We will discuss how to build a highly effective business funnel that starts with the content you create on LinkedIn, moves to attracting followers, and then moves them off of LinkedIn to deliver results for your business.

Dr. Pelè

SERVICE OVER SELLING

In the 1990s I wrote and produced six out of the twelve songs for Alexander O'Neal's EMI major label album, titled *Lovers Again*. The album was featured at #29 on Billboard[11] magazine's Hot R&B chart and one of my songs, 'Let's Get Together', was the lead single. In those days, in my youth and inexperience, I felt I had made it because I received a production advance from a major record label and got some press. But then suddenly the artist was dropped from the label and the money soon ran out. I eventually left the music industry because without ongoing marketing, the record stopped growing in the marketplace. I quickly found myself having to make new career decisions to sustain my young family.

Before you conclude this is just a pity party, I want to let you know that the real lesson I learned from that era of my life was not about what I *didn't* get from the music business. Quite the contrary, it was about the incredible gifts I would receive over and over for the next several decades until this very day.

You see, every quarter, in my mailbox, I would get (and still get) a check with royalty payments from those songs I wrote more than twenty years ago. I jokingly refer to it now as 'mailbox' money, but the technical term for those payments is *royalties*.

This kind of business model has taught me so much about what works and what doesn't in business. I have since become hooked and forever sold on the idea of investing in things today that will produce assets so I can reap greater rewards tomorrow, versus seeking to collect as much as I can now, in the present.

This is the difference between service and selling.

With selling you reap rewards if people buy what you're selling *now*, and those rewards will last only for as long as you continue advertising and selling. With serving and helping people, you are investing in them by creating content *assets* that will reap rewards—like royalties—over time.

In his highly celebrated book, *The Ultimate Sales Machine*, the late Chet Holmes[12] showed the difference between the short game—selling—and the long game, service. He explained the idea that only 3% of the people we meet in the marketing and sales process are ever ready to buy right *now*. The challenge here is that most of us end up focusing and selling ONLY to that 3% when in fact there is at least another 67% of people out there who are available to buy later, if only we would stop selling to them, and start *serving* them.

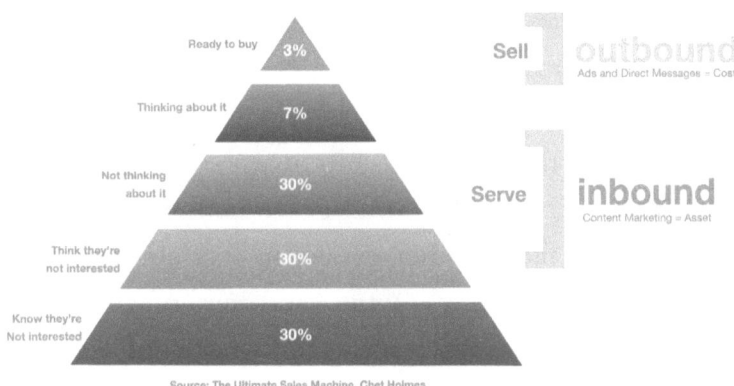

When we shift from outbound selling (advertising and direct messaging) to inbound serving (content marketing), we are investing for the long term.

I see this play out in so many ways on social media. In my practice, I get so many people reaching out to me, telling me that they heard of my work from a podcast, or blog, or video content they consumed somewhere. Sometimes I'll get a new paying client purely because they learned about me through work I created online over the years. This is why I like to say, *content creates clients*—just like royalties—long after the work of creation and publishing has been done.

The shift from selling to serving is perhaps one of the most important paradigm-shifts we can make. We will discuss more about how to implement content strategies that will continue to pay dividends long after they've been produced.

FACT OVER FICTION

For far too many people, content marketing is a strategy of 'hope'. I like to call it 'spraying and praying'. Here's the scenario: you put out your content and then you sit back and hope that someone will see it, consume it, and perhaps decide to do business with you someday. The difficulty with this approach is that it usually produces one thing only: *crickets*.

It's truly a fiction and a fantasy to invest so much effort into something and then merely *hope* you'll get something in return. You need to follow the facts as they evolve so that you can develop some kind of data visibility—some modicum of certainty—by seeking to understand what's working and what's not.

One of the greatest quotes attributed to the late, celebrated management thinker Peter Drucker is the following simple statement:

"If you can't measure it, you can't improve it."

While there is some debate as to whether he said those exact words or not, the truth in that quote is self-evident. How can you proactively improve something you're not measuring? How do you know you should slow down in a car if you never know how fast you're driving? The fact is you can't manage what you can't measure. You can't drive forward with blindfolds on.

I like to call the things you're measuring 'facts'. They present themselves without dispute because we can see for ourselves how things are working. You can count how many times people react, comment, or follow your content back to your website. These facts need to be the things that drive decisions, not a hope in some idea that 'perhaps' someone will see your content someday and respond to it. We need to have facts—not *fiction*—at our fingertips to set the right course for delivering content marketing success.

The idea of quantification, of implementing a culture of measurement, is actually more elusive than it sounds. When it comes to content marketing, you'd think there is data everywhere on social media and that measuring the impact of your content should be easy. Well, it turns out that what most social platforms provide is not organized in such a way as to help you quickly gather *meaning* from all the data your content generates. Sure, you can see how many reactions, comments, and views you get on a single post, but it's not much use to you if you can't quickly answer simple questions like, "what's my best (or worst) performing post this month?"

In the next chapter, we will present in full detail, the 3R principles for building Relationships, Reach, and Results. In that conversation, you will discover the central role and importance of analytics and why it is a cornerstone of our software and community, ClientJam.

The bottom line is this: if you are to be successful in attracting your ideal clients, you will need graphs, tables, and other analytical tools to know exactly what's working and what's not in your content marketing efforts. The path to great business decisions and results is made possible by data visibility.

Having said that, let's jump now into the details of the 3R Principles of Social Velocity!

3. The 3 Principles For Landing High-Value Clients

In order to help you find, keep, and grow your ideal clientele, we have taken a sometimes insurmountably difficult business development process and simplified it down to three memorable principles. After years of working with our community of clients, we have been able to summarize into these three principles the fundamental *strategies* and *tactics* that range from getting started on social media to consistently attracting, converting, and serving high-value clients.

To move you into implementation gradually, we've separated strategies from tactics. In this chapter, we'll begin by describing overall strategies, and then in the next section, we'll go much deeper into each principle's tactics. This way, we stay faithful to both, as the wisdom of Sun Tzu aptly implores:

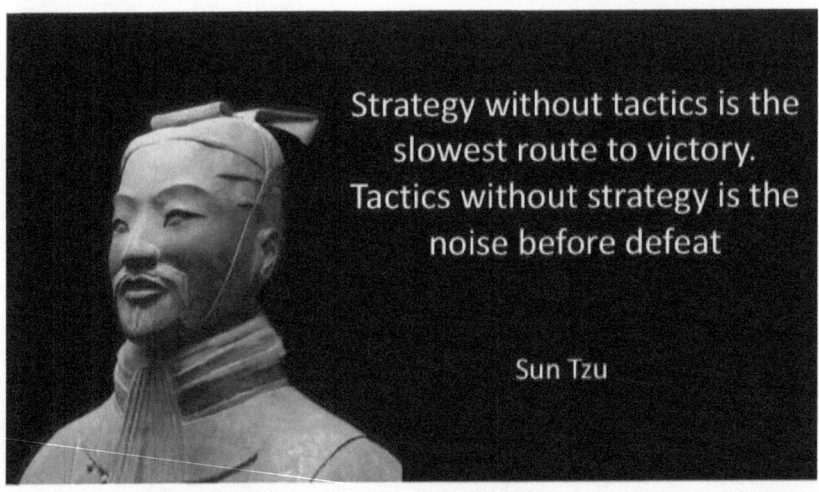

The principles, strategies, and tactics we describe herein are not in dispute. They are proven and supported by years of research, implementation, and optimization. Of importance is the fact that these principles are not proven exclusively by our firm or our clients. They are in fact the same general principles you'll learn from any business school, see implemented by thought leaders, or find in practice at any of the world's most successful companies. The heavy lifting we've done is to demystify content marketing and organize it into the 3R principles of *Social Velocity*:

1. RELATIONSHIPS
2. REACH
3. RESULTS

You can think of the 3Rs of Social Velocity as a three-legged stool. You need each one working effectively or else the entire stool—and its occupant—will fall. You could also think of the 3Rs as a set of three independent, critical processes that are intertwined, as we depict in our diagram here. Each process feeds into the next one with important requirements that keep the process of getting high-value clients moving forward:

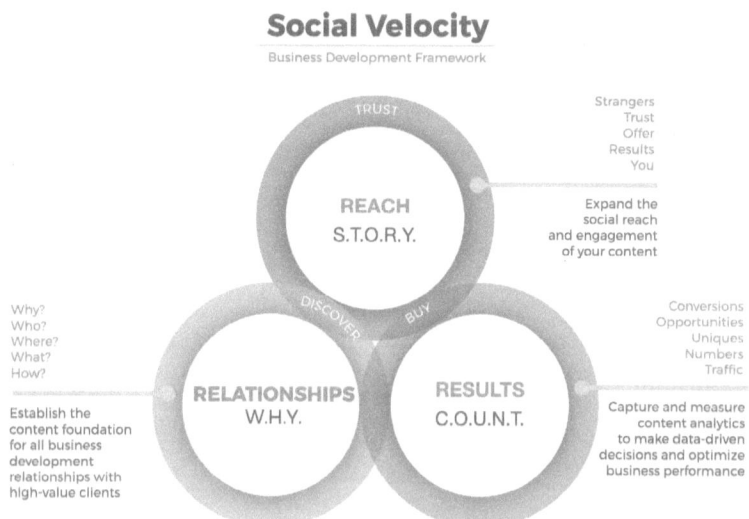

Finally, you can think of Social Velocity as what happens when content marketing serves the purpose of ***moving*** high-value clients toward you. Remember that the main difference between speed—i.e. hustling—and velocity revolves around movement in a specific direction. That being said, here is our definition of Social Velocity:

"Social Velocity is the effective use of content to build RELATIONSHIPS, extend the REACH of your brand, increase business RESULTS and MOVE your highest-value clients to discover, trust, and buy from you."
— Dr. Pelè

In the next section of this book, we will go into the tactics for launching each of the 3R principles. Right now, let's go ahead and jump into a general introduction of the overall system.

SOCIAL VELOCITY PRINCIPLE ONE: RELATIONSHIPS
—You Can't Catch A Whale With A Worm

In nature, there are rules in play at all times. One of the more interesting ones I've discovered is that large whales feed on some of the smallest animals in the ocean, particularly tiny plankton and some worms species, but they must have *tons* of it at a time.

Imagine the folly of a fisherman learning this and then trying to catch a whale with only one tiny, single worm? This is how I describe the folly of trying to attract high-value clients with these speedy, annoying, spammy mass-marketing efforts. You need to build something deep, wide, and lasting. You need to build relationships.

The engine of any good business is its people, and people do their work in the world through relationships. Without good relationships, there can be no business. This is why the very first consideration for anyone seeking to start, grow, and sustain a business concern is how they will find, keep, and grow mutually beneficial business relationships. This is also why we have to get off the hamster wheel of 'speedy' client acquisition strategies—and focus instead—on developing relationships.

One of our earlier clients, we'll call him 'James', is an intellectual property expert. For many years he struggled with how to create his online presence and tell his story in a way that would build relationships with his ideal clients. Like many of us who seek clients online, he had spent thousands of dollars on courses, trying to find a magic solution. When we began working with him, our advice was to discard all of the technology funnels, spammy introductory video emails, and all the other speed-and-hustle-based strategies he had learned through various online courses. We asked him instead to slow down and build relationships. Why? Because in the end, that's what *business* is: mutually beneficial relationships between buyers and sellers.

Once we helped him craft a LinkedIn profile 'makeover' and created a more 'relationship-based' approach to his marketing and sales, he closed a $150,000 deal on the strength of deepened business trust. The initial value we exchanged created great velocity in his business and its impact is still visible for him today.

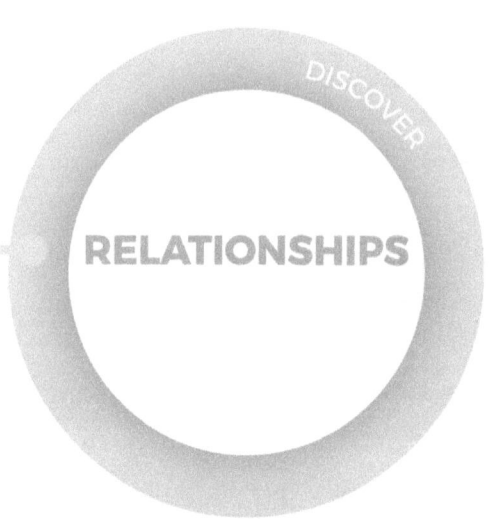

Establish your content foundation so that your high-value clients can discover you, trust you, and eventually buy from you.

The purpose of the Relationship section of the 3R System is to help you prepare a basic foundation for getting *discovered* by your highest-value clients. When people discover you, the relationship is voluntary and can flourish without the fear of sales in the introductory phase. Suffice to say that getting prepared for high-value business relationships will involve questions around the nature and purpose of your business, as well as your unique approaches for creating client results, all of which should be easily understood from your LinkedIn profile.

Understanding and clarifying the foundation for building your business relationships is an important first step in the 3R system.

SOCIAL VELOCITY PRINCIPLE TWO: REACH
— Going Fast Won't Get You Far On A Hamster Wheel

In the early days of ClientJam, one of our clients—let's call her Jane—gave me a most powerful testimonial when she first joined us. She had been meticulously tracking the progress of her LinkedIn posts after joining us, and she sent me a message asking for a Zoom call. Here's what she said on the call, with a high degree of excitement:

"After launching my new content strategy with the 3R System, one of my posts has seen 800% increase in popularity!" - Jane.

I asked her to tell me what her strategy for acquiring clients was *before* she turned to content marketing and Social Velocity.

"Connection requests," she said. "I would send out up to one hundred requests per day, being careful to stay under LinkedIn's radar. It rarely worked. People would report me as someone they didn't know, and I actually got my LinkedIn account restricted a couple of times."

"Sounds like you were running fast," I suggested.

She nodded; her eyes opened extra-wide.

"Sounds like you were *really* going fast," I repeated, seeking to drive the point home, "but not very far!"

We both laughed, enjoying the moment.

I was so thrilled with her good news that, after a long discussion and verification of her analysis, I felt it was important to really dig in and document how she did it. What Jane implemented was the simple paradigm shift we discussed earlier, which top LinkedIn influencers understand well:

Instead of random connections, focus on building thought leadership that earns you followers.

If you switch to this business development strategy, it will mean that 80% of the time, you'll be SERVING, not SELLING. You'll be building and expanding the social reach and engagement of your content. In the end, you'll be seen as a trusted advisor by those who choose to follow you.

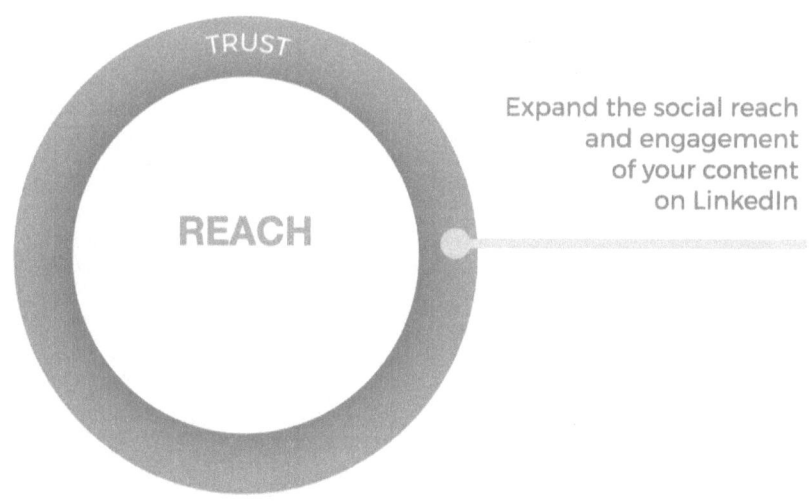

The path by which a high-value client travels from not knowing who you are to eventually buying something from you comprises both technology and psychology. We have identified five stages of this journey, which we see as an evolving S.T.O.R.Y. (story) in which your high-value client is the hero. Moving them from one phase of this story to the next is the true power of content marketing.

Your goal is to move your ideal prospects from people who are *Strangers*, to people who *Trust* you, to people who are ready to consider your *Offer*, to people who are willing to partner with you as clients to create *Results*, and then finally to people who are happy to tell others the good news about working with *You*.

In section two we will go deeper into the tactics of what we call a S.T.O.R.Y. funnel.

SOCIAL VELOCITY PRINCIPLE THREE: RESULTS
— You Can't Drive With Blindfolds On

For many years, at least until the slogan was retired in 2002, Apple has been known as the 'think different' company. In fact, many still believe that it was this mantra, handed down by the great Steve Jobs, that is primarily responsible for how Apple became the world's most valuable brand.

Well, yes, and no.

The real reason for Apple's success can be traced to when they made a shift from releasing designs based on the talents, skills, and beliefs of their engineering teams, to making product and business decisions based on big data analytics about their customers' behaviors. Once they began focusing on what their customer *results* were showing them, they were able to join Google and other data-driven companies to learn, through behavioral economics, what was working, and what was not.

The simple strategy of making decisions based on knowing what's working and what's not can dramatically improve your business.

For example, everyone talks about gaining *authority* in the marketplace. Yet, very few people are involved in counting and monitoring the *process* and *pivots* required to gain that outcome over time. The truth is that outcomes are usually out of your control, but quantification of your activities and a consistent review of analytics (quantification + review = measurement) are the best ways to ensure you're doing more of what works, and less of what doesn't.

In the early 2000s, I was involved in a marketing campaign that has become one of the greatest business parables of my life. I worked for EDS at the time, as the global Director of Marketing. In that role, I was part of a team that delivered the now legendary EDS Airplane advertisement, which you can probably still find through a Google search.

In that ad, we made the simple point that building a business is like building an airplane while it is flying. Sound hard? Well, that's how business works! You are always in motion, and the only way you can make certain decisions is to get the analytics and feedback you need—in real-time—to answer the questions that drive your business.

This is why it is so important to *count* what you're doing while you're doing it. Results help us answer the questions that help us build our businesses. Only by looking at our results can we answer questions such as these:

1. How effective are my social posts, according to my analytics?
2. What should I do more of, and what should I stop doing?
3. How can I optimize my content marketing for both the short and long term?
4. What are we learning about the types of posts, articles, videos, or other media that are getting the best engagement?

5. What is the Social Velocity of my content marketing?

Without data, none of these questions can be answered. And without answering these questions, you cannot optimize or improve your content marketing. As Peter Drucker (may have) once said, you'll be unable to improve that which you do not measure.

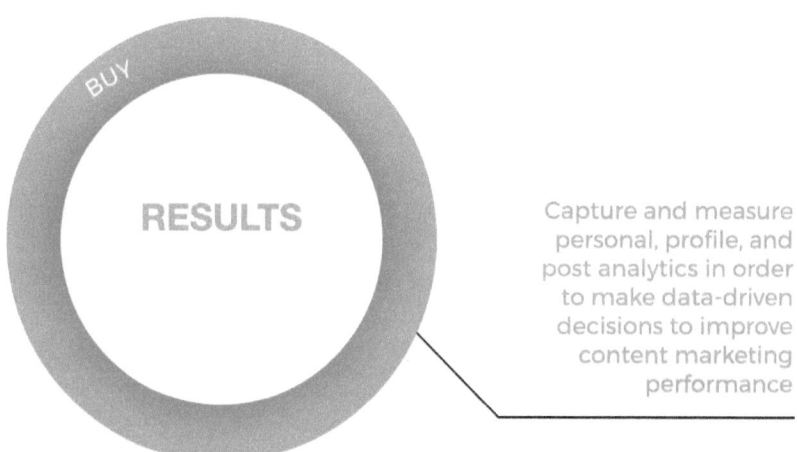

We will discuss the details and tactics around what we need to measure over time, such as *conversions*, *opportunities*, *unique* followers of our brand message, our *number* of leads, and our overall *traffic*.

WHEN YOU'RE READY TO START

In the next section of this book, we will be diving into greater details and tactics for *how* to implement the three principles. If you've gotten this far, I congratulate you! We've already shared a lot of data in just one medium, the written (or spoken) word. In truth, I believe in the age-old mantra that we learn best by *doing*. As such, we have developed software and a community of practice that will be your companion for learning and implementing the 3Rs.

That software and community is called *ClientJam*, and it will help you build business relationships, increase the reach of your content, and leverage analytics that will help you improve your content marketing results over time.

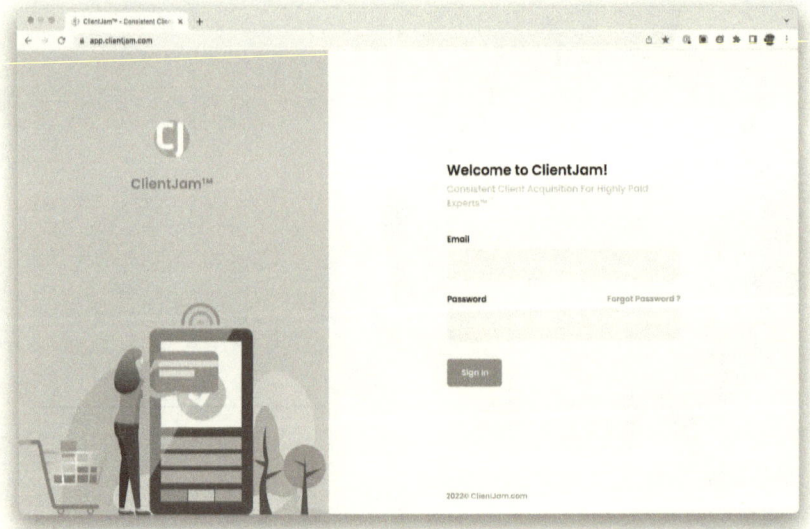

When you feel ready to get started with the details of the 3R System, I would encourage you to create a free account at ClientJam.com, where you can follow along and answer the questions that will follow each chapter of Section Two. By answering these questions and applying what you're learning, you will go a long way toward creating and implementing a content marketing strategy that will help you find, keep, and grow your ideal clientele.

Consider the following approach as you read through the coming chapters:

1. Read each chapter and brainstorm ideas for the strategy and tactics of *your* Social Velocity content marketing plan.
2. Answer the questions at the end of each chapter on ClientJam.com to create and document your Social Velocity content marketing plan. When you create an account and complete the short training on ClientJam, you will find a button in the Training section labeled 'My Plan', which is where you will capture your unique answers for how you plan to implement Relationships, Reach, and Results in your content marketing.
3. Complete the training and share your 'My Plan' section with work colleagues, supporters, or friends. Get their feedback as you prepare to move forward to execute your Social Velocity content marketing plan.

With the power of the Internet and its plethora of tools, there has never been a better time than now to get started with content marketing. As the saying goes, the journey of a thousand miles begins with one step. This is that one step right here.

With only 1% of LinkedIn users actively creating and sharing content, this is a great time to get started so you can connect with more of your ideal clients.

In the next two sections of this book, we will discuss how to leverage Relationships, Reach, and Results to create Social Velocity, which will help you find, keep, and grow your highest-value clients.

Ready? Let's go!

Dr. Pelè

SECTION 2:
GETTING SOCIAL VELOCITY

Social Velocity

4. Principle One: RELATIONSHIPS

Whenever people are in motion, whether they are in a car, a plane, or just walking down the street, it is easy for them to consider the *speed* at which they are traveling. What is not always obvious is that, if they are moving in a specific direction, then the actual quality they are engaged in is *velocity*.

Speed can be achieved in one location if you're on a treadmill. You can be going extremely fast but getting nowhere. Same thing with a hamster on a hamster wheel. When we think about the way we build business relationships in terms of speed versus velocity, we get two very different approaches and outcomes.

If your goal is to get clients *fast*, you can use all the tricks and shiny objects you want to help you automate and speed up the process, but you may end up getting nowhere because most people you approach want relationships to grow naturally and safely. In this paradigm, it is easy to end up with a lot of speedy business development activity that amounts to 'much ado about nothing'.

If, on the other hand, you want to go *far* in a business relationship, you would consider more carefully the elements that make *starting* a good relationship possible. And the key element you'd consider is the differentiating element between speed and velocity, which is *movement*. Are my prospects moving closer to me? Is my *content* moving them closer to me?

Social Velocity is achieved when you ensure that everything you do with your content is creating the slow and steady movement of a prospect toward a buying decision in your favor.

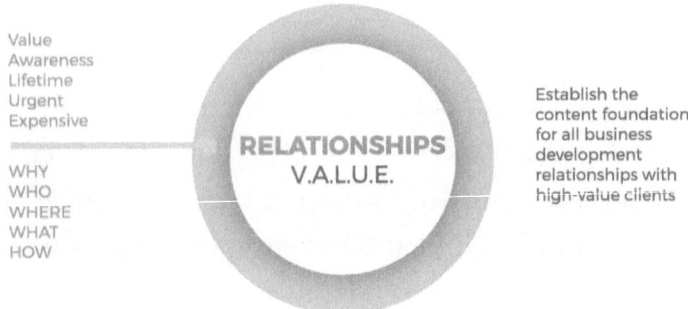

In this chapter, we will discuss the Social Velocity strategy and tactics you will need to build business RELATIONSHIPS with high-value clients. To kick off that discussion, let's start with one of my favorite stories: *The Parable of W.H.Y.*

THE PARABLE OF W.H.Y.

Once upon a time, the Turtle and the Hare decided to get high-value clients on LinkedIn, the big, sleeping elephant in their jungle. They both created accounts and began populating their profiles with the information they thought would best promote their brands to ideal clients.

Dr. Pelè

The Hare's profile read something like this:

"Quick! Click here; buy all my stuff now!"

The Turtle's profile read something like this:

"I help folks like you get the stuff you want."

Already you could see a difference. The Hare was focused on himself and speed. The Turtle was focused on others.

The race started. The Hare took off immediately, hustling forward with great speed, installing browser extensions and automation tools that he felt would surely give him an advantage. The plugins promised to get him up to 75 connections per day, with multiple follow-up direct messages. This meant he would be getting about 1,000 new connections per month. *Wow*! Talk about speed!

This was awesome, he thought, except, it was also *unethical*. It was against the LinkedIn elephant's terms of service.

The Turtle plodded along slowly, lagging far behind. He didn't use any automation or browser plugins. He simply started writing posts that were helpful to his intended audience. He told stories about how his ideal clients found solutions to their problems. He engaged with everyone who commented on his posts and he measured how people engaged with his content over time.

In the end, he only got a few new connections, but something else was happening. He was building relationships with his existing connections and gaining followers from people outside his connection base. Because only 1% of LinkedIn's approximately 740 Million members[13] were posting content regularly, his posts stood out. He was delivering real value through his content and engaging in insightful business conversations with his first-degree connections.

Suddenly, the great LinkedIn elephant woke up! He saw immediately all the spammy stuff the Hare was doing. Without wasting any time, he caught the Hare and restricted his account with a chokehold, instantly putting him to sleep.

While all this was happening, the Turtle kept plodding along, deepening relationships and attracting followers merely by telling stories and being helpful. As he arrived at the final bend in the road, strangers started approaching him, asking if they could sign up for his courses and services. Observers, paparazzi, and connections alike were sending him likes, comments, and encouragement, chanting:

Slow and steady wins the race!

Right before the Turtle crossed the finish line, Hare got up and made one last, mad dash forward, but he was overly encumbered with all his automation, plugins, and the bad karma he had developed when so many people reported and blocked him on LinkedIn. Try as he did, he just couldn't catch up with the slow and steady Turtle.

The race ended as the Turtle crossed the finish line.

Speed lost.

Social Velocity won the race.

The next day, a video shot by one of the paparazzi was on the front page of JNN (Jungle News Network). It showed an anxious journalist shoving a microphone in the Turtle's face, asking, "How did you do it?"

The Turtle answered with an air of confidence the world had never associated with him before:

"Every high-value prospect is asking a question in their mind; and that question is W.H.Y., "why hire you?" I knew what my customers needed. I knew their problems and I talked about them everywhere with my content. I simply answered their question W.H.Y." — Dr. Turtle, Austin, TX, 2021

BUILDING YOUR FOUNDATION ON W.H.Y.

The key to success on LinkedIn is to answer the most important and inescapable question in your ideal client's mind: W.H.Y.?

Why hire you?

What problem—specifically—does your ideal client have that you can solve? Once you know the answer to this question, you can use it to establish a focus and foundation upon which all future business relationships will be successful. It's like building a house. If your foundation is weak, the facade and everything else will crumble.

In our parable, the Turtle had the right foundation. He was focused on building relationships, engaging positively with others, being helpful, and providing value with his content. He knew exactly what his clients were searching for and 'W.H.Y.' they would want to hire him.

Too many of us are like the Hare, disorganized, without a plan, and looking for the fastest route to business success. In fact, according to 2021 research from the Content Marketing Institue[14], more than half— 57%—of business-to-business marketers do *not* have a documented marketing plan!

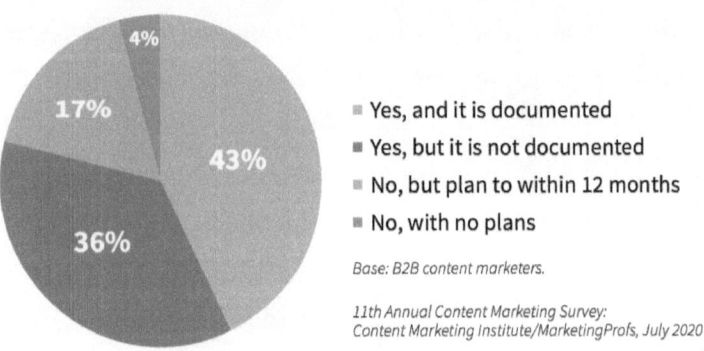

Because we lack a plan, we are too easily drawn to the latest shiny objects being marketed as 'the next big way to get clients' on LinkedIn. Sometimes we may even be seduced into using tools we know are against LinkedIn's rules, such as automation, bots, and browser plugins. All without having a strong, intimate knowledge of 'W.H.Y.'

In the end, Social Velocity starts and ends with people—real people—coming together in real business RELATIONSHIPS. And in any relationship, each party has to know what the other wants and why the relationship stays successful. In the absence of that kind of clarity, the relationship will either never start, or fall apart too soon.

There is an Igbo (West African) saying that goes like this:

"Onye ajuju adigi efu l'uzo."

Translated, it means:

"The traveler who asks questions will never be lost."

To create a content marketing *plan* that can be executed successfully on the journey of client attraction, one must similarly ask and answer several foundational questions. If we don't have answers to these questions, we will be lost along the way.

Also, every good plan must be documented. As such, to begin executing these answers, I recommend writing them down. When we work with clients, we have them log into ClientJam and document their content marketing plans in the same environment they'll be using to execute them. This way, both strategy and tactics are housed in the same location for easy access:

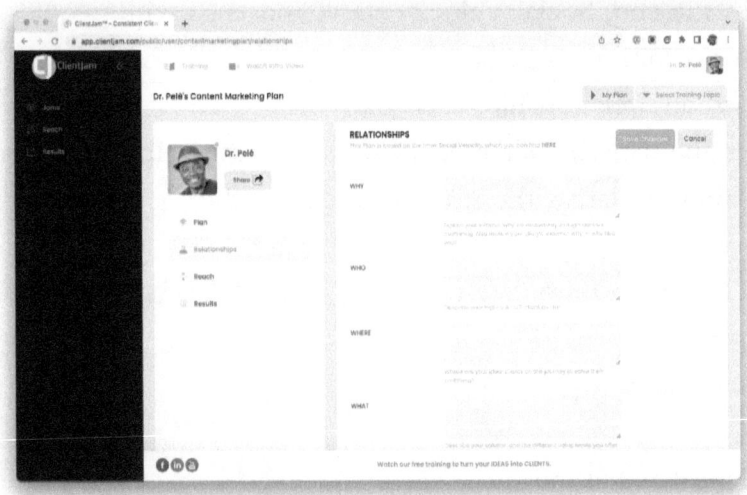

In the RELATIONSHIPS section of our overall content marketing plan, there are five key questions we must answer:

1. Why?
2. Who?
3. Where?
4. What?
5. How?

In the next few chapters, we will take a look at these questions individually and use our answers to fill out our content marketing plan and LinkedIn profile, the foundations for all of our future business relationships.

CHAPTER 4: ACTION ITEMS

1. Visit ClientJam.com and create a free account. Once you log into your account and complete the training, you will find a 'My Plan' page in the Training section. Perform the following actions to begin creating your Social Velocity content marketing plan.

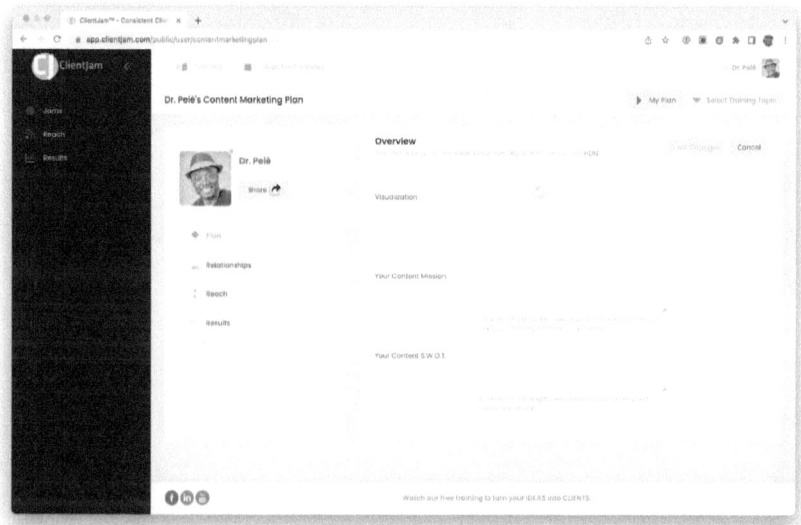

2. *Visualization:* Upload an image that will help you visualize the success outcome you seek from the results of your content marketing. It could be personal or professional. Anything that helps you come alive and visualize your success.

3. *Your Content Mission:* Document the purpose, objectives, and desired outcomes of your Social Velocity content marketing plan.

4. *Your Content S.W.O.T.:* Document the strengths, weaknesses opportunities, and threats of your plan.

5. Why?

The first question to answer for your ideal prospect is the one they will think of when they first visit your LinkedIn profile or website 'home page'. The content you present there—which will be the first impression and basic foundation for all future business relationships—must answer the question W.H.Y…

… *why hire you?*

This question of 'W.H.Y.', needs to be answered from two perspectives.

1) *Why do YOU do what you do?*
2) *Why should anyone hire YOU for what you do?*

The first perspective is the *internal* one. If you want to build relationships of value on LinkedIn, you should start by asking yourself why you do what you do, not *how* you do what you do.

Have you noticed how most people seem to respond to the question, "what do you do?" by talking about what and how they do what they do? For example, they usually say something like, "I am a teacher." (Their title or *what* they do). And if you probe further about what kind of teacher they are, they will tell you *how* they do what they do. Now, there is nothing inherently wrong with these kinds of answers, except they completely miss an opportunity; people need to know WHY you do what you do. As Theodore Roosevelt once said:

> *"No one cares how much you know until they know how much you care."*
> *- Theodore Roosevelt*

If you want people to stop, look, and potentially care deeply about what you do, tell them why you do it. As Simon Sinek explains in his book, *Start With Why*, it's important to begin with WHY, not only because that is your source of inspiration, but because it becomes your best tool for inspiring the rest of us.

So, how can we leverage this in our content marketing? Simple: I like to say that your internal WHY—your purpose—also happens to be your best source of great *content* as you move forward to market your business. If you leverage your WHY—the things that inspire you—to create content, you'll never run out of ideas for your content marketing.

Now, for the second, *external* perspective;

W.H.Y. should anyone hire you?

As the Turtle said in our parable earlier, every potential customer is walking around with this one single question on their mind and they will only stop to pay attention if you directly and immediately answer it in your profile and in every piece of content you share over time.

This is perhaps the most important question in all of business because it gets at the heart of exactly what your ideal clients want.

To begin answering this question, log into ClientJam and document this in the Relationships tab of your 'My Plan' content marketing plan form:

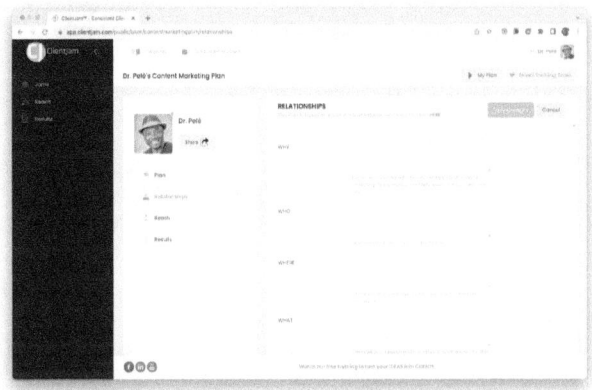

Here, you have to carefully map your expertise to the challenges people currently need to solve in the world. Next, you need to write it all down. If you don't write it, you won't use it. And if you don't use it, you'll lose it!

In my example above, I have the two answers to my WHY listed as:

- *My purpose is to spread profitable happiness ... (internal)*

- *I help business owners attract their highest value clients on LinkedIn ... (external)*

By providing these two answers—concisely and with clarity—you are now ready to develop a content foundation for being discovered by your ideal clients. Without this kind of clarity in your profile and content messaging, no one will stop to learn more about what you do on LinkedIn.

CHAPTER 5: ACTION ITEMS

1. Visit your 'My Plan' page on ClientJam.com.

2. Reflect on your thoughts and insights from this chapter and consider how you will use them to continue creating your Social Velocity content marketing plan.

3. In the 'WHY?' section of the RELATIONSHIPS tab, explain your internal 'why' for innovating through content marketing.

4. Now, in the same box, also explain your external 'WHY?' Concisely explain why your ideal, high-value clients should hire you above the competition.

6. Who?

Perhaps the next most important question in all of business (besides every other 'most important' question, right?), is: WHO? *Who is your ideal client?*

The reason this question is so important is that in the absence of its answer you don't know who you're selling to! As Lewis Carroll is credited with writing in Alice In Wonderland, "if you don't know where you're going, any road will take you there."

"If you don't know where you're going, any road'll take you there"
~ Alice in Wonderland

The only problem is that—in business—taking any road other than the specific one that leads to your ideal clients is a recipe for disaster.

To be successful in landing high-value clients you need clarity, a plan, and a system that will both *attract* and *repel* different groups of people according to your plan. The ones you repel are those 'tire-kickers' that would waste your time and not pay you what you're worth. The ones you attract are the ones who will pay you well, appreciate your work, and refer you to others when your work is complete.

To arrive at total clarity on this question, you need to step into the *story* of your ideal client. This is the narrative they are living in right now, where they are the hero (this story is never about us. It is about our high-value clients exclusively). Once you understand and can empathize with them, you can then begin to determine if they fit the profile of your ideal, high-value client.

WHO EXACTLY IS A 'HIGH-VALUE' CLIENT?

With all the business buzz words and phrases on social media, why should you care about this one? The reason is centered around the word 'value'.

Most of us are aware of phrases such as ideal clients, customer avatars, buyer profiles, or customer personas. While they all generally mean the same thing, an injection of the word 'value' provides a whole new way to think about your clients. It gives you a way of measuring not only if a customer is a good 'fit' for you, but also how important they are to your business in both the short- and long-term. If you aren't able to provide measurable value to a prospect, or if a prospect does not check the boxes in terms of needing the 'value' you provide, then they should be taken off of your list.

Since we're placing such high value on the word 'value' (pun fully intended), here's an explanation of what a high-V.A.L.U.E. client must have, be, and do:

- VALIDITY: High-value clients will decide to work with you based on the validity of the outcomes you provide, not the price you charge. This implies that you must communicate the validity and value of outcomes, not merely price.
- AWARENESS: They have a high awareness of the specific, identifiable problem they have a desire to solve. Their difficulty is that they do not understand the strategy or possess the technology for solving that problem, which is where you come in.
- LIFETIME: They can be retained (or will return) over time and a lifetime-value (LTV) calculation can therefore be reliably made and measured.
- URGENT: They have a strong, urgent, time-based need to solve their problem, which requires their immediate action.
- EXPENSIVE: The problem they have would be very expensive to them in the absence of your solution and they are willing to pay a premium to solve it.

If a prospect doesn't check these boxes, then they will not be a high-value client for you and your relationship with them will most probably end up being difficult.

THE P.A.I.N. ANALYSIS

Next, we need to conduct what I call a 'PAIN' analysis on the demographics and psychographics of your ideal client. It's a play on the well-known SWOT analysis used in designing business strategies. Instead of analyzing the state of your overall business, you're analyzing what you understand about your ideal prospect.

The PAIN analysis will give you the basic building blocks for the kinds of content you should be sharing with your prospects over time.

First, write down everything you know about the demographics and psychographics of your ideal client avatar:

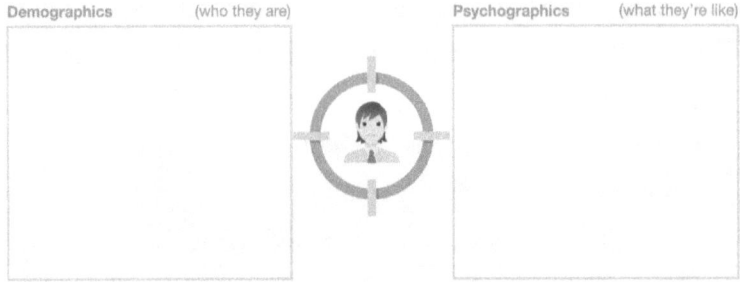

Next, step into the story they are experiencing in their lives. Document what you believe to be their current, internal pain and aspirations, as well as their future, external nemesis, and imagined outcomes.

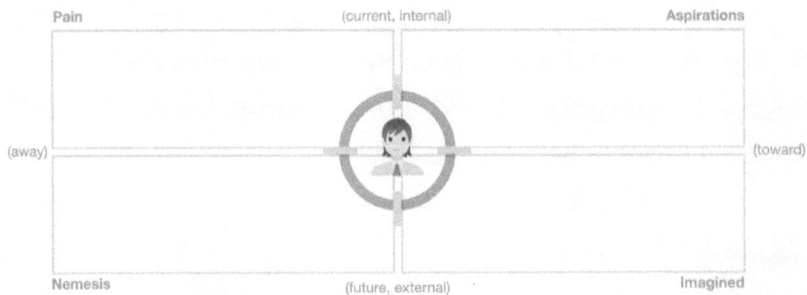

The top-left quadrant is where you describe your ideal prospect's number one pain. This needs to be something that keeps them up at night and should be a current problem that is internal to their business. What are they currently experiencing within their business? How is it affecting them personally and professionally? Whatever you capture here should be something they are looking to get away from.

In the top-right quadrant, consider what their internal (personal and professional) aspirations are. This is more about feelings than tangible outcomes. One great icebreaker question I love to ask my prospects is:

"When you look forward 12 months from now, and you're doing a happy dance because you've found the success you seek, what do you see? What do you feel about yourself and your business at that time?"

I've found the 'happy dance' question to be a fun way to help people describe what they are moving toward on an emotional level.

In the bottom-left quadrant, write down their external nemesis. If you think of internal aspirations as something they are moving toward, think of their external nemesis as something they're running away from. One common example with a lot of my clients is time. They find themselves always under the pressure of time. They feel as though they don't have any time. Time is, therefore, a future, external threat that can work against them, because if it isn't managed well, it could derail many plans.

Finally, in the bottom-right quadrant, describe the visible, tangible success outcomes they are seeking. Again, they are running away from the things they hate, such as the time it takes to do their marketing, but they are moving toward an outwardly visible and measurable success in the future. These could be personal or professional goals and accomplishments.

Once you've completed your brainstorming, log into ClientJam and summarize all the information you have about 'WHO' your highest-value clients are.

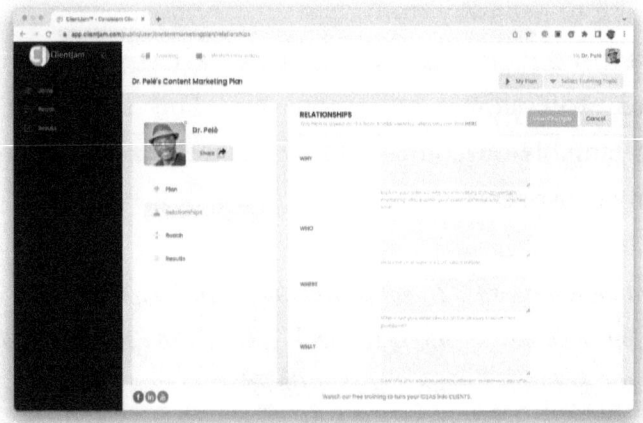

CHAPTER 6: ACTION ITEMS

1. Visit your 'My Plan' page on ClientJam.com.

2. Reflect on your thoughts and insights from this chapter and consider how you will use them to continue creating your Social Velocity content marketing plan.

3. In the 'WHO' section of the RELATIONSHIPS tab, describe your High-V.A.L.U.E. client avatar.

7. Where?

In the previous question about 'who' your ideal clients are, we talked about placing yourself empathetically in their shoes and experiencing the story they are living through. We call that story your client's journey. It is the journey your client must take—with or without you—to arrive at their intended destination.

You could think of this journey as the gap between an 'A' state and a 'B' state. A 'hell' and a 'heaven'. A 'once upon a time' and a 'happily ever after'. The key is that you need to describe this story, compartmentalize the steps in the process, and then understand fully 'WHERE' your ideal clients are in that journey so that you can speak empathetically about it in your content and meetings with them.

Let's look at the following example of your client's journey:

Start by defining where your ideal client was before they met you. That state is the 'A' state. Next, write down what life would look like when the business problems—the ones you can solve—are successfully addressed. That is your 'B' state. Finally, segment the journey into 3 phases and 9 sections. Give each phase a title, such as 'No clients', 'Course development', and 'Client funnel'. This could represent the 3 big phases they have to go through to create an online course. Next, within each of the 9 sections, describe what specific business challenge needs to be solved to advance to the next section.

This gives you a format upon which you can map out your client's journey and discover—or predict—where they are in that journey. Not knowing where your ideal client is in their journey will leave you constantly guessing what their needs might be and your content will not be cohesive and organized.

On the other hand, knowing *where* your clients are in their journey of success is just as important as knowing what problems they have in the first place. You can use what you know to consistently provide helpful information and engage them in conversations that *move* them closer to you.

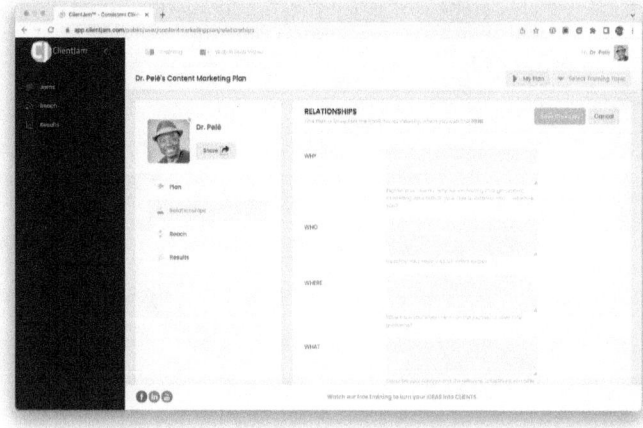

Once you've completed your brainstorming for WHERE your clients are in their journey, log into your 'My Plan' section of ClientJam and summarize all the information you have about them into the 'WHERE' text area of the Relationships tab.

CHAPTER 7: ACTION ITEMS

1. Visit your 'My Plan' page on ClientJam.com.

2. Reflect on your thoughts and insights from this chapter and consider how you will use them to continue creating your Social Velocity content marketing plan.

3. In the 'WHERE' section of the RELATIONSHIPS tab, describe where your ideal clients are on the journey to solve their problems.

8. What?

Now you are ready to document and design exactly 'WHAT' your product and service will be. As we've mentioned previously, far too many professionals *start* here. They start by defining products and services only to wake up one day and discover there is no demand for what they've built. Nothing hurts as much as working hard for months on websites, branding, videos, and all kinds of promotional materials, only to discover that no one is interested or willing to buy what you've created.

So, what will your product be? How will you create a product and service that works harmoniously with your ideal prospects' buying process?

The answer is to roll out your products and services 'slow and steady'. By this, I mean, first, give a lot of value through helpful content, but frequently let your audience know that they can learn more and get further help either for free or at a low price point outside of LinkedIn. You could call this a 'minimum viable offer' and it should partially solve your client's problem. Once enough of your ideal clients show up and demonstrate that this relatively inexpensive offer is valuable, then you offer them the full service or product that completely solves their problem.

I call this the 'Crawl-Walk-Run-Product-Ladder' and it follows the logic of a child growing up.

Crawl, Walk, Run

First, a child must learn to crawl, and only after that will they be ready to walk. And only after learning to walk a bit, will they be able to run. This natural evolution is critical. If you try to get a child running before they can crawl or walk, you can imagine the potential disaster you may create!

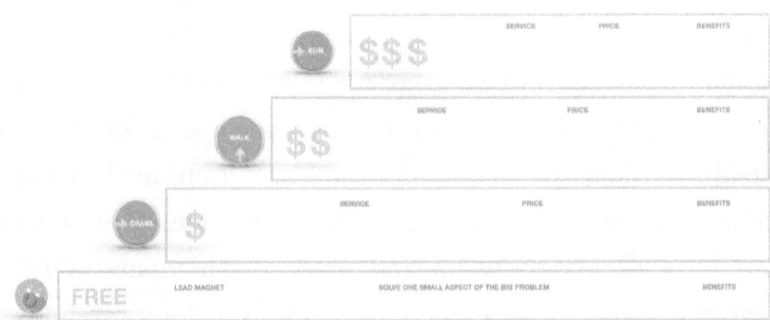

First, offer free content on LinkedIn, then move your clients through calls-to-action (CTAs) into a low-risk, 'crawl' phase where they can see what level of value you are capable of providing. After that, you present them with buying options at the 'walk' or 'run' levels, depending on where they are in their needs and buying process.

Once you've completed your brainstorming for 'WHAT' your product levels will be, log into ClientJam and summarize what you have so you can use it to clearly communicate how you can help your high-value clients.

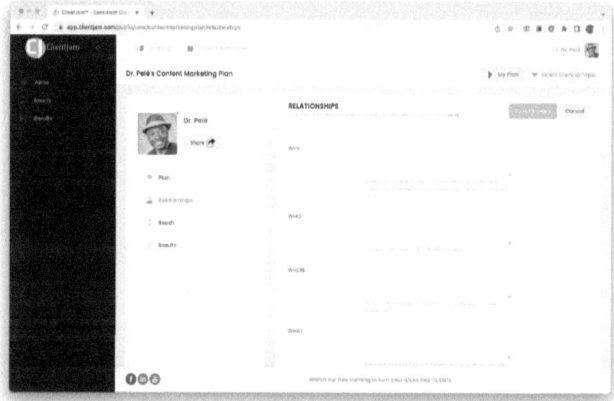

CHAPTER 8: ACTION ITEMS

1. Visit your 'My Plan' page on ClientJam.com.

2. Reflect on your thoughts and insights from this chapter and consider how you will use them to continue creating your Social Velocity content marketing plan.

3. In the 'WHAT' section of the RELATIONSHIPS tab, describe your solution and the different value levels you offer.

9. How?

Finally, it is time to clarify exactly HOW you solve your ideal high-value client's problems. Notice that we save this question for last because there is an inherent danger with it. As human beings, we tend to be biased to the things that we find most important and necessary. However, the truth about business relationships is that—at first—our clients usually do not care about exactly *how* we solve their problems.

In the business development process, the first thing they care about is whether or not you *can* solve their problems.

When clients do get around to caring about the question of 'how' you might solve their problems, the next set of questions on their minds is how you compare to their *other* buying options.

The best way to use the question of how you solve a client's problem is in the context of handling objections and addressing competitive concerns. You want to be able to position in the minds of your ideal clients the idea that you—and you alone—can uniquely solve their problem in this or that specific way.

Let's face it, you are probably not the only coach, consultant, or business owner in your niche that your clients have been exposed to. They, therefore, need clarity and a sense that—in their story—you are the ONE guide they have been waiting for.

To brainstorm the question of 'how' you solve customer problems, we use what I call a '5Cs story plot' with both indicators of where your client is in their story on the one hand, and the transformations you bring (uniquely) on the other hand to move them to the next step in their story of success.

The 5Cs are a shorthand I developed to help visualize the various stages of any story. Every story, whether it is in our lives, or in business, or in a movie, has some variation of the following phases:

1. *Context* (where we are today)
2. *Challenge* (the problem we need to solve)
3. *Change* (the change we create with our solution)
4. *Climax* (the success we achieve from our solution)
5. *Close* (the conclusion and 'moral' of the story)

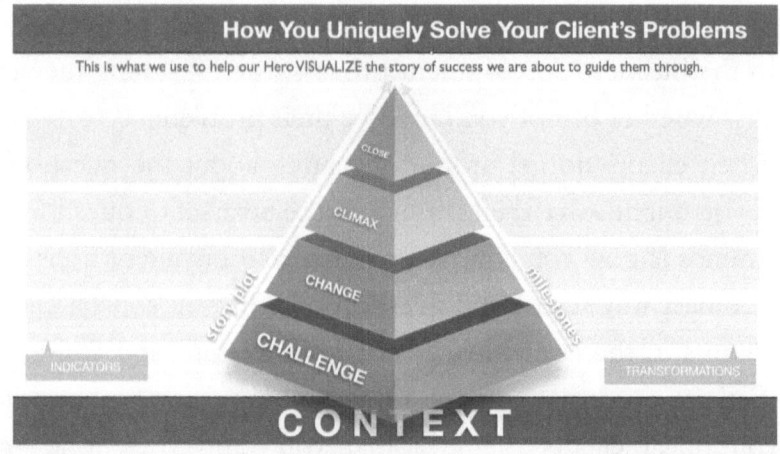

At every step in the story, we then describe the 'indicators' that would confirm for us that our client is in that stage. (We could use the information we gathered from the previous WHERE questions to help us fill in the blanks here). At each point in the client's developing story, we are ready to talk about HOW we uniquely bring transformation to move them along to the end of the journey.

By doing this, we fully map out how we identify and solve problems and especially, how we do it uniquely and powerfully vis-a-vis the competition. When we answer these burning questions in the minds of our ideal clients, we are growing their trust and *moving* them toward a buying decision in our favor.

Once you've completed your brainstorming for HOW you will uniquely provide value and solutions at each stage of your client's buying journey, log into ClientJam and summarize your answers.

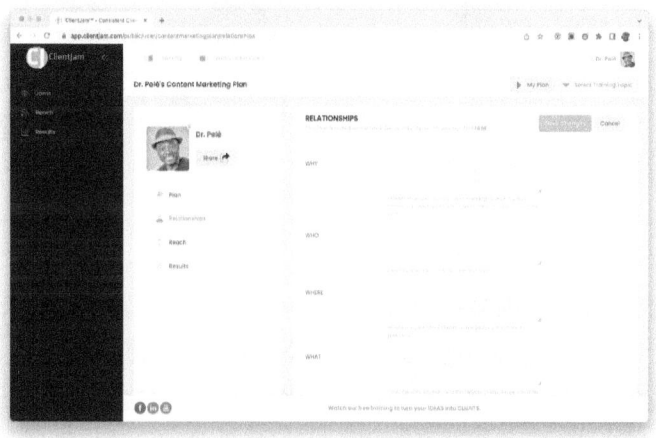

BRINGING IT ALL TOGETHER ON LINKEDIN

Your LinkedIn Profile and website are the final destinations for all the answers you've developed in this section. Remember one rule: you have 5 seconds to either keep the attention of a visitor or lose it!

Let's take a look at what a completed profile should look like and analyze the different sections:

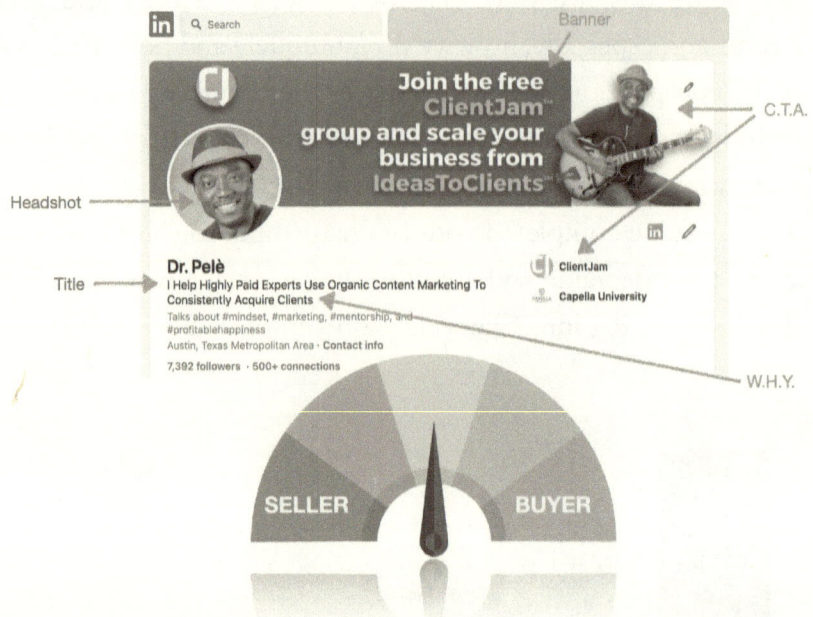

1. ***Use the buyer-to-seller continuum*** to judge every section of your LinkedIn profile and website by whether or not you're talking about yourself (the seller), or your high-value client (the buyer). If you're talking about yourself, change it to talk about your buyer. Remember, people are focused on themselves and their problems, not us.
2. **Banner:** this is your first and best opportunity to make a positive impression on a visitor to your profile. Far too many people either leave it blank or put information there that is talking only about themselves. Heat maps have shown that, besides the picture, the banner is usually the thing people see first. Make your banner function as an 'advertisement' and call-to-action without being too 'salesy'.
3. **W.H.Y. Statement:** It is important to have this in your banner. Make sure to check what it looks like on mobile so

that it is legible on all platforms. Insert your statement that answers the buyer's question, *why hire you?*

4. ***CTA (Call-To-Action):*** This will provide a destination for your potential clients. It should point to the top of whatever funnel you're working on, whether that is a lead magnet, a webinar, or an email opt-in of some kind. Make sure that your current company is the same as where the CTA is pointing.

5. ***Headshot:*** your picture should be professional and the same one you use everywhere on social media. We will discuss later the importance of being seen as the same consistent person wherever your ideal clients go.

6. ***Title:*** your title area should not be used to display your business title, such as CEO, Vice President, etc. This is a holdover from the original purpose of LinkedIn as a resumé database. Nowadays, as more people use LinkedIn as a business-to-business networking hub, the truth is that your title is no longer as important as what you can do for people. So, either repeat a version of your W.H.Y. or talk about your customer's journey here. This is prime real estate for getting attention before people are attracted away by another shiny object online.

7. ***The Summary (About) Section:*** The about section is where you tell the story of your client, not of yourself. Again, most people use LinkedIn as a job resumé board. When people read your summary, it can't be a long lecture about how great you are. Unfortunately, no one cares, at least not yet! Below is an example of what mine looks like. Notice that the first paragraph is designed to get attention so that people will click and read below 'the fold'. Following that, notice that I am NOT talking about myself. Instead, I've

stepped into the story of my ideal clients and I am building an empathetic connection with them. Once I have that connection, I would have earned the right (at the bottom) to provide a call-to-action to my products and services.

Here is an example:

ABOUT

▶ HOW DO YOU STAND OUT FROM THE CROWD ONLINE? If you've ever wondered how to get past the noise, attract your ideal clients, and build a highly profitable business using social media, READ ON …

Here's the reality: no matter how excellent your product or service, it is of no use to you if no one ever discovers you, likes you, or trusts you enough to buy something from you.

▶ CONSIDER THESE QUESTIONS:

— How much time gets wasted crafting the perfect posts and articles only to get a handful of views, likes, and comments?

— How do you translate your genius into profitable business relationships, increased authority, and differentiation as a thought leader?

— How do you position your brand, content, and social presence so that your highest-value clients come to YOU and not the other way around?

▶ HERE ARE SOME ANSWERS:

If you're a company, consultant, or creative entrepreneur what you need is to expand the reach and results of your content marketing.

— Grow your audience and increase your influence on LinkedIn without being 'salesy'.

— Create powerful content with organic reach that gets seen by more of your potential clients.

— Use efficient technology and ethical processes to find, keep, and grow your ideal client base.

If you want to expand the relationships, reach, and results in your business, then you need Social Velocity™ — which turns your content into conversations that create clients.

▶ HERE'S HOW I CAN HELP:

1. ClientJam is software and a community that helps you deliver engaging content and track post analytics so you can build your brand, grow your tribe, and win high-value clients with Social Velocity.
2. PodcastAgent is a (Done-With-You) podcast and video production service that helps you convert your passion and expertise into content marketing results.

3. Social Velocity is an action-learning, 1-1 Mentorship course that will help you leverage the power of LinkedIn and content marketing to significantly scale your business.

▶ WHAT OTHERS SAY:

"Dr. Pelè is my go-to, 1-1 Marketing Mentor! He helped us close a $150,000 deal within 30 days of launching!" - Matt W., CEO

"ClientJam is a game-changer for my business!" — Cheryl J., Author & Coach

'Dr. Pelè taught me the psychology and technology of online marketing, which put me on a path to 6-figures in my very first year." - Jon S., Consultant

▶ WANT TO LEARN MORE?

Let's talk:

https://drpele.com/call

CHAPTER 9: ACTION ITEMS

1. Visit your 'My Plan' page on ClientJam.com.

2. Reflect on your thoughts and insights from this chapter and consider how you will use them to continue creating your

Social Velocity content marketing plan.

3. In the 'HOW' section of the RELATIONSHIPS tab, describe how you uniquely provide solutions vis-à-vis your competition.

4. Print and share the completed RELATIONSHIPS section of your Social Velocity content marketing plan with trusted collaborators for feedback and discussion.

5. Visit your LinkedIn profile and update it using 'The Buyer To Seller Continuum' approach we've described in this chapter.

10. Principle Two: REACH

We've talked so far about the differences between our villain, speed, and our hero, velocity. However, until this section, we haven't yet introduced our major reason for *why* velocity matters. Understanding the power and purpose of velocity as our aspirational analogy is of critical importance because it is the best way to earn trust—and high-value clients—on social media. Let's do that now.

Velocity measures the motion of an object in terms of how fast it's going *and* how far it is displaced, meaning the object has to start in one place and end up in another. Speed, on the other hand, tracks how fast something is going and can be measured with no location change or displacement whatsoever.

The reason we measure velocity in physics is so that we can predict when an object will arrive at a future (different) location. For example, if you're running out of gas on a trip and want to travel from your current location to the closest gas station, knowing your velocity (speed and direction) will help you predict precisely when you'll arrive at that gas station. Knowing your speed alone will not help you because you could be traveling in an entirely wrong direction, away from the intended gas station.

Another example might be two trains mistakenly placed on the same track. If both are traveling at a velocity (speed and direction) that brings them *toward* each other, we know we'll be in danger of a pending collision, which we can calculate for and avoid. Similarly, if we know that both are traveling at a velocity (speed and direction) *away* from each other, we will know that we are safe, and there will be no collision. Now, imagine if *only* the speed of these two trains was available to us. Without the knowledge supplied by direction and displacement, we would not know if we were safe or in danger, and we would have no idea of when—or if—there will be a potential collision.

Now, let's bring this analogy back to the world of people, social media, and business development.

Think of your LinkedIn connections—the people you know—as your current *reach* or 'circle of influence'. Consider what would happen if you were able to consistently attract new *followers*, people currently outside that circle of influence. The greater the 'distance' you expand that circle of influence in a 'direction' away from the center, the more opportunities you open up for meeting new people who could potentially become ideal clients for you in the future.

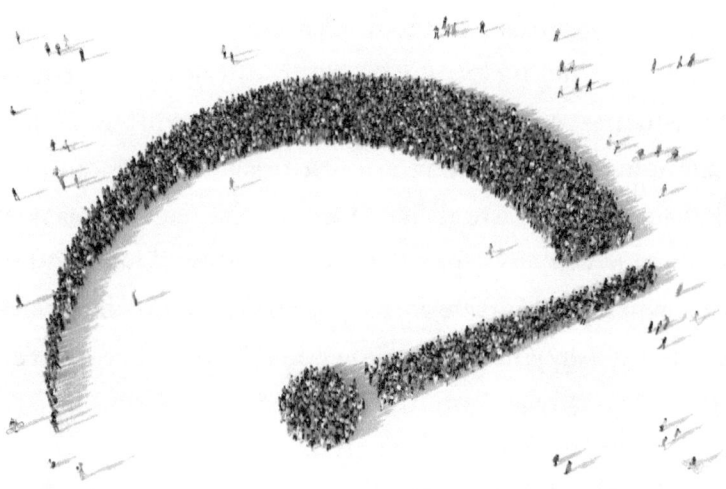

If you never increase your Social Velocity by widening your circle of influence, you'll most probably remain in a kind of quiet, painful obscurity with few if any new client opportunities.

REACH is an estimate of how much you're expanding your circle of influence and therefore, your potential to gain new, ideal clients.

In social media, reach is usually measured by looking at how many people actually *viewed* your content (versus how many impressions were sent to them by the social media platform). If you want to have a sense of when and if you will gain enough traction online to meet more potential prospects you currently do not know, you've got to have a way to measure your 'reach' as a key performance indicator (KPI).

As with our previous examples regarding the use of velocity in physics, only a knowledge of social reach can help us know if we are in danger or moving toward business development success. Here are some reasons why understanding reach is so important:

1. Knowing your reach allows you to understand what's working and what's not in your content marketing.
2. You can plan ahead and fine-tune your messaging and content to respond to what you see as the impact of previous content releases.
3. You can improve your return on investment (ROI) with respect to how you spend resources on different kinds of content campaigns.

Social Velocity is achieved when you know that you are steadily expanding your reach and creating more opportunities to find, keep, and grow new ideal clients.

To achieve an expansion of reach, your main tool will be your *content*, and the technology by which it reaches your audience over time is what I call your S.T.O.R.Y.

In this chapter, we will review the S.T.O.R.Y. process of turning *Strangers* into people who will come to *Trust* you, who become ready to receive your *Offer*, who will become clients for whom you create *Results*, and who will eventually refer *You* to others. Using this approach, you can build trust in the marketplace of ideas and earn more followers and potential clients over time.

Now let's dive into an examination of the power of marketing reach from one of the most important (and real-life) parables I've been fortunate to experience first-hand, *the Music Business*.

MARKETING IS THE NEW PRODUCTION

In the early 1990s, I took the bold step of pursuing my passion as a full-time singer, songwriter, and music producer in Minneapolis, Minnesota, the home of Prince, Flyte Time, Funkytown, and the

Minneapolis Sound. Like most musicians back then, I was consumed by the pursuit of quality in my product—the *music* of music—but I was not very knowledgeable about the *business* of music.

As things would turn out, I found success as a songwriter and producer at Funkytown, a professional studio operated by Steven Greenberg, known internationally for writing the 1970's hit, 'Funkytown'. Over time, I collaborated with several members of Prince's band, such as guitarist Mike Scott, his bassist Brown Mark, and members from his groups Mazarati and The Time. At the height of it all, I produced 'Lovers Again', a #29 Billboard-charting album for legendary R&B crooner, Alexander O'Neal, who was the original singer of The Time.

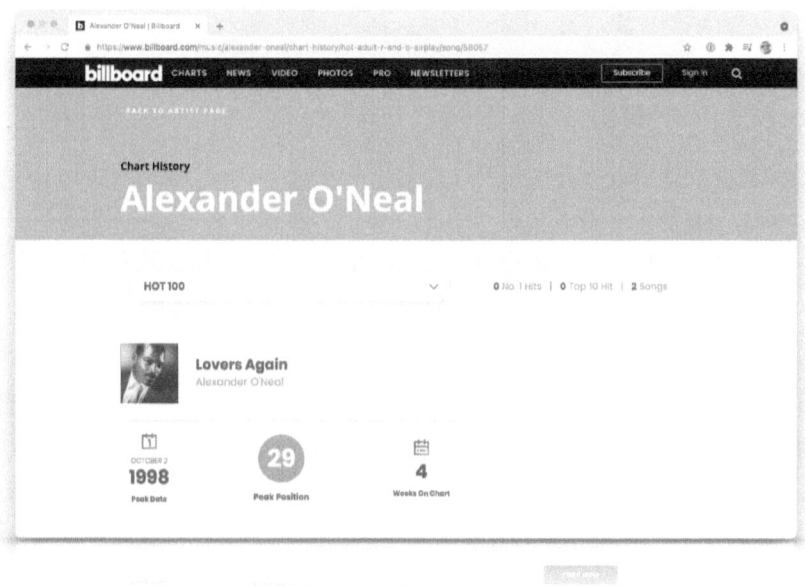

I thought I had made it in the music business!
Until I realized I hadn't.

Within a few weeks of Alexander O'Neal's album release, he got dropped from his label, EMI Records, for professional challenges unrelated to his new album. I was devastated!

In one instant, the record I produced was removed from its major-label marketing engine and left to its own devices. It immediately tumbled down the charts into obscurity and never regained momentum. Most fans of Alexander O'Neal today would be surprised to discover that record was ever made. Without the marketing engine, it was silenced. No one heard of it again.

This was when I learned perhaps the simplest but most important business lesson I've come across:

Great content is useless if no one ever hears or sees it.

I learned in that moment that true success in music—or in any business—requires a 20:80 effort split. 20% for MAKING your product, and 80% for MARKETING it.

The problem most of us face is that we have it the other way around. We spend 80% of our effort working hard—privately—to create products, services, content, and so on. And thereafter, we spend only 20% of our time and effort marketing it before we give up in despair.

The idea of *instant* success because one had a record deal was now exposed to me as the myth it truly was. To make it in the music business without the power and money of a record deal, you would need to master both making great content and the art of publicly using that content to create a following, a process which is certainly not instant.

Armed with my newfound wisdom, I've since flipped my understanding of the production process. Regardless of industry, your greatest effort doesn't end with the production of your product. It *starts*! The rest of the production process involves sharing your product with people and getting marketing REACH for your it. What most of us understand as 'production' must be expanded to include marketing. In some ways, I now believe:

Marketing Is The New Production.

Without marketing REACH there is no movement of value from producers to consumers or sellers to buyers. If you want to be successful in today's online—public—social landscape, you have to first become *known* for something. From there, you build relationships, gain trust, and create clients.

Most people would agree with my assertion here. However, the lingering question is usually this: in today's noisy, overcrowded social media landscape, how exactly *do* you get reach for your content?

The answer is found in what we introduced earlier as a S.T.O.R.Y. funnel. You share an ongoing story of value to your marketplace over time. The story you tell combines psychology, technology, and business development phases. And yes, you guessed it: It's a memorable acronym too! Your S.T.O.R.Y. is the pathway by which reach is achieved and measured. Your ideal clients follow this pathway toward you, and not the other way around.

THE SHIFT FROM PRIVATE TO PUBLIC

I was once in an introductory meeting with 'Jim', a one-time highly successful corporate executive. He explained to me that despite his many years of success, he had been 'aged out' and couldn't find work as an employee any longer. At 50+, he was embarking on a different career path to coach others, and he suspected—correctly—that his ideal clients were on LinkedIn. This was all well and good, except he seemed to believe he could keep doing the same things he'd been doing in his past corporate experience and expect different results.

"How do you plan to get clients on LinkedIn?" I asked.

"I plan to keep working my Rolodex," he said. "I have deep corporate relationships and connections on LinkedIn from my many years as a senior executive."

"That seems to be a rather private, network-based strategy," I said. "How has that been going so far?"

"Not so good," he said.

"How so?"

"So far, none of those connections have introduced me to people who need my coaching service."

"And why might that be?" I asked him, continuing my Socratic questioning to help him arrive at answers by himself. After a few rounds of my directed questioning, he lit up and with a knowing smile, said:

"I see where you're going with this! If I want to expand my influence beyond the world of employment, I will need to target and earn new followers!"

"Precisely!" I said. "You'll have to come out from the private boardroom and become a public persona. You can't earn new followers in secret!"

He was shaking his head. I could just imagine his thoughts swimming in the direction of the new set of behaviors he would have to employ to build a new, more public brand on LinkedIn.

"Simple as this may sound," I said, "you can't keep knocking on the same doors and expect to see different people behind them!"

Before our conversation, Jim's circle of influence involved only his existing corporate connections. Certainly, he had deep relationships with powerful company employees, but he soon discovered that he couldn't leverage their influence beyond the companies they worked for. As an employee in a company, one can use good political skills to create success, but I helped Jim understand that in the open market of ideas and strangers, one needs a *public* strategy that will earn new followers consistently over time.

Jim has since moved on to be one of our most passionate content marketers. He has earned a large, loyal following on LinkedIn, and although it took a while, now when he posts an opportunity to help people, prospects come to him, instead of the other way around.

THE S.T.O.R.Y. FUNNEL

The Social Velocity strategy Jim used to expand his reach and earn new followers on LinkedIn is what we call a S.T.O.R.Y. funnel. The acronym stands for:

1. Strangers
2. Trust
3. Offer
4. Results
5. You

A S.T.O.R.Y. funnel is a multi-phase process through which your marketing content is experienced. Think of how a movie theater, or home television, or smartphone, or computer, or any other media device can convey a story. Each medium provides a

Social Velocity

different type of experience. In the Social Velocity S.T.O.R.Y. framework, we have five experiences, which match five different psychological and relationship levels a prospect has to go through in the *story* they are experiencing to become your client:

1. They start by being *strangers* to us.
2. We can then move them from being strangers to people who *trust* us enough to want to learn more about us.
3. Once they are in our community of trust, we make our *offer* known to them.
4. When they've accepted our offer and become clients, we are on a trajectory to create excellent *results* with them.
5. When excellent outcomes have been created, they become willing to refer *you* to others.

Content and technology are the vehicles that move your audience through your funnel from 'strangers' to 'you'. And both are powered by *psychology triggers*, intentionally embedded in all of your messaging.

In Robert Cialdini's seminal book, *Influence*[15], he identified several psychology triggers that have been adopted widely on the internet today. These are the foundational triggers of persuasion he identified:

1. **Consistency** (people align with their commitments)
2. **Liking** (people work with people they like)
3. **Authority** (people defer to experts)
4. **Reciprocity** (people repay in kind)
5. **Unity** (people respond well to shared identity)
6. **Scarcity** (people want what they can't have)
7. **Social Proof** (people follow the lead of similar others)

Most people who use these triggers on the Internet do so either through instinct or by copying what they see others doing. Rarely do people systematically and strategically use psychology triggers for each marketing or sales campaign message. However, they should, because it greatly increases the predictability and effectiveness of marketing and sales campaigns.

Over the years, on top of Cialdini's original list, I've identified several additional triggers, and the most powerful of them all, is the psychology of *story*. Here are the ten psychology triggers that I've identified:

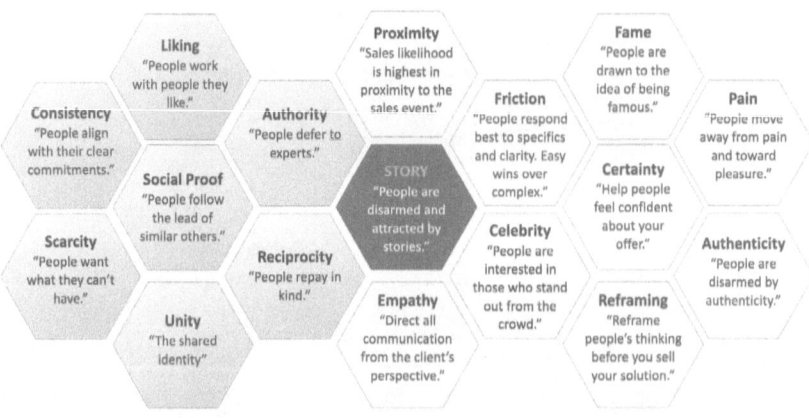

1. ***Proximity*** (proximity increases sales likelihood)
2. ***Friction*** (people respond best to simplicity, and clarity)
3. ***Fame*** (people are drawn to becoming famous)
4. ***Pain*** (people want to move from pain to pleasure)
5. ***Authenticity*** (people are disarmed by authenticity)
6. ***Reframing*** (people respond when beliefs are changed)
7. ***Certainty*** (people respond well to confidence)
8. ***Celebrity*** (people are interested when you are known)
9. ***Empathy*** (people listen best when you talk about them)
10. ***Story*** (people are disarmed and attracted by stories)

In the next chapter, we will take a look at each of the five stages of your S.T.O.R.Y. funnel.

11. Strangers

At the beginning of any story, we learn about the *context* within which the hero is existing. In that context, the hero is a stranger to us, until we see things happening around them through which we learn their name and other circumstances important to the story. We aren't able to care much about the hero until we learn more about them.

Similarly, in the story of how your ideal, high-value clients come to you, they begin as strangers. It's important to remember that, as strangers, we can't expect them to care much about the things we care about unless they learn more about us in a very natural, unforced way.

At this stage in the relationship, your goal is simply to get *known* by your ideal prospects in such a way that you don't scare them away with an over-eagerness to engage. (Remember, slow and steady wins the race!) Once they know you, your next goal will be to grow their trust, which is the second stage of the S.T.O.R.Y. funnel.

Far too often, consultants, advisors, and coaches make the very human mistake of being so preoccupied with their desire to move the sales ball forward that they talk far too much about themselves. We call this 'verbal vomit'. What's worse is that some people will propose a decision meeting at the very first encounter. That usually doesn't work very well, especially for high-value clients, which is why I like to say, "never propose marriage on a first date."

A *stranger* in our system is someone who is not yet a 1st degree connection of yours on LinkedIn, meaning they are either 2nd-degree connections (connected to your 1st degree connections) or 3rd-degree connections (connected to your 2nd degree connections). Once you identify a stranger you want to bring into your S.T.O.R.Y. funnel, there are several strategies for moving them closer into your circle of influence. Here is a non-comprehensive list:

- Send a Connection Request
- Share original content so they can engage with it
- Follow them so you can begin engaging with their content
- Send a direct message
- Ask for referrals
- Join Groups to discover new people
- Paid Advertising
- Holding Events

Let's take a look at how some of these strategies stack up in terms of effectiveness. Below is a diagram I call the Social Velocity Quadrant, where we show the relationship between the three principles: Relationships, Reach, and Results.

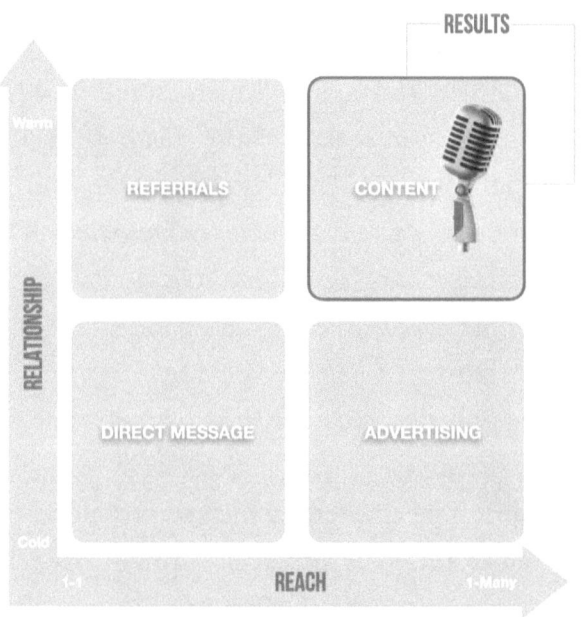

In the diagram we see that on the Y-axis, we are showing RELATIONSHIPS, which can range from cold, to warm. Clearly, we want our relationships to start as warm as possible.

On the X-axis, we see how REACH can go from non-existent (1-1), to very far, (1-many). Again, the preferred outcome is to have our marketing reach as many people as possible.

Now, let's place a few of the strategies we have discussed into this diagram. First, you will find that Advertising is good for getting our message to many people at once, which is a good thing when done well. However, besides the fact that it can be extremely expensive, it is not a great strategy in terms of relationship warmth because we remain strangers to the people we attract and still have to do the heavy lifting of warming up those relationships.

Next, you will notice that Referral Partnerships are extremely warm on the Relationship axis but extremely low on the Reach axis. This makes sense because we all know how powerful referrals can be. The only challenge with them is we can't guarantee when they will happen and can't do much to control the process.

Now, let's look at Direct Messaging, which is the absolute worst strategy for building trust at scale because it is both cold in relationships and low in terms of reach. Again, we can all understand how off-putting it is when a total stranger tries to sell you something through a direct message. What's worse is that this strategy has been so completely abused by automation tools that are all against LinkedIn's terms of service. Bots and automation tools for direct messaging only deserve a mention here as a warning that you should *never* use them.

This leaves the option of Content, which stands alone and is high in the Results quadrant. It is the sweet spot for turning strangers into people who trust you. Content is both high in relationship warmth as well as possessing the potential for a 1-many reach, especially when you leverage LinkedIn's algorithm to do it.

According to the Demand Gen Report[16], 95% of B2B consumers say content helps them trust a business more, so as a core strategy for growing your influence, it is a no-brainer.

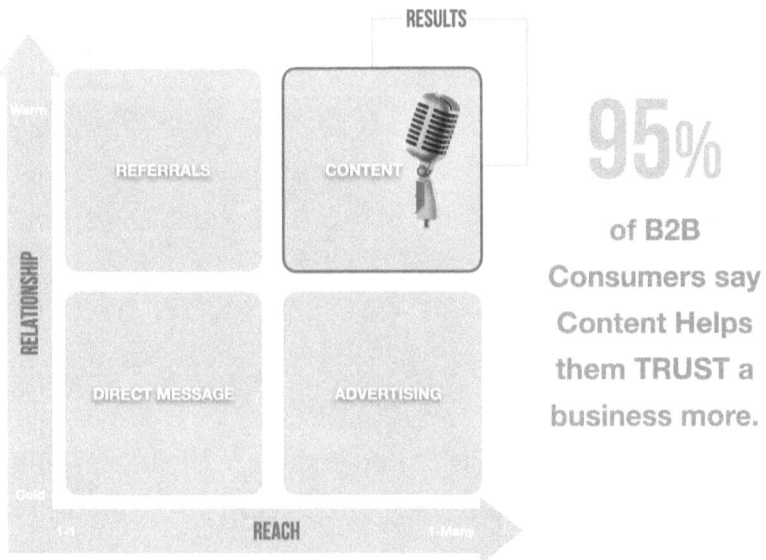

Content is indirect, non-invasive, and can be entertaining, inspiring, educational, or all of the above at the same time. Content helps people decide to follow you on their own terms, so that's where we must begin if we want to grow their trust.

Do some brainstorming to determine what your 'Strangers' phase content strategy will be. Once you have some ideas, log into your ClientJam account, and enter them into your Content Marketing Plan in the 'Reach' section.

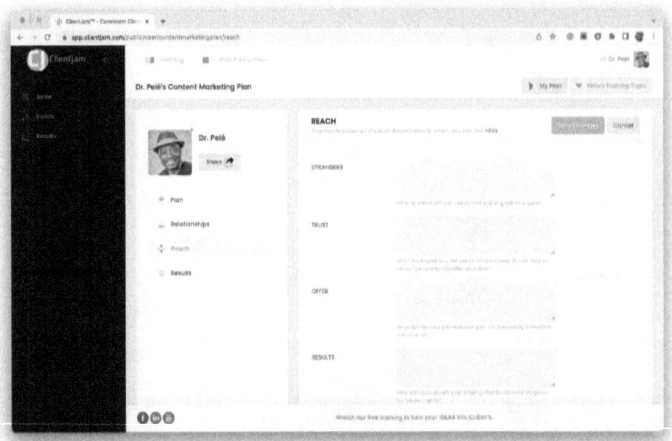

Now, let's take a look at the second stage of the S.T.O.R.Y. funnel as well as how we can leverage LinkedIn's algorithm to take our content as far as possible.

CHAPTER 11: ACTION ITEMS

1. Visit your 'My Plan' page on ClientJam.com.

2. Reflect on your thoughts and insights from this chapter and consider how you will use them to continue creating your Social Velocity content marketing plan.

3. In the 'STRANGERS' section of the REACH tab, describe what psychology and technology systems you will use to find and engage strangers.

Social Velocity

12. Trust

Every story has a ***challenge*** phase right after we meet the hero, where we learn about the status quo and whatever troubles the hero is currently experiencing. It is here that we get to know and empathize with them.

Similarly, after an initial business introduction to Strangers, the ultimate destination of the relationship we launch must be Trust. To achieve trust, we have to do two things: build rapport and transform people's existing beliefs about potentially working with us.

One of the best ways to do this is to share content in which you adopt the role of trusted advisor, teacher, interested party, or sympathizer in all future interactions with prospects. Once a prospect enters your LinkedIn community, your goal is to build enough trust through content to drive them to a high-proximity encounter with you. This encounter could come in the form of a webinar, an evergreen presentation, or even a short, introductory meeting, depending on what's appropriate based on how you met the prospect in the first place.

Accompanying the education or engagement you provide should be a healthy dose of empathy, where you demonstrate that you understand your prospects' challenges, aren't asking for anything, and that you truly, genuinely care. As the saying goes, people care about you when they know you care about them.

However, building trust is not only for 1-1 interactions. It is also for building your brand and expanding your circle of influence overall. Successfully moving people from the Strangers phase to the Trust phase is one of the most important steps for creating Social Velocity reach.

Once you have people in the Trust phase, you will have to continue sharing helpful content and exchanging messages with them until such a time as it becomes appropriate to invite them off of LinkedIn for either a one-on-one conversation, or an evergreen presentation you may want to share with them.

One of the things we've learned at ClientJam is how easy it is for people to feel a bit overwhelmed with creating new content ideas. You could call it a form of 'writer's block'. What we've found is that one of the biggest reasons for running out of ideas is because we tend to get most of them from our own experiences and expertise. If you go back to The Buyer To Seller Continuum, you'd see that most of that type of content is about us, the sellers. But as we know, it's not about us. No wonder we run out of ideas!

Also, when we do talk about our buyers, we're overly focused on the latter part of their journey funnel where we hope they are ready to make a buying decision. We therefore don't create enough content to support the earlier parts of their journey funnel (where more of them exist). We need to balance our content to reflect the entire buyer's journey.

To fix this challenge, we've developed a module called 'I.D.E.A.S. 365', a way of creating content that is focused on our buyers. Specifically, we've created five categories of ideas and aligned them with the psychological buying stages of a typical client's journey toward us. Before a buyer says 'Yes' to our offer, they will typically go through the following stages:

I.D.E.A.S. 365	
Interest	Prospects first become aware and interested
Desire	They want to learn more
Educate	We provide ongoing education
Action	We allow them to 'try' our offer
Sell	We present our offer and they make a decision

Notice that these stages form the acronym 'I.D.E.A.S.' (yes, we love acronyms...they help us remember stuff!) The powerful thing about categorizing ideas in the same buckets that represent your buyer's journey is that you are orienting yourself toward thinking about *them* and their challenges, not just yourself. Also, this allows you to balance your content for all stages of the buyer's journey.

When using this strategy, it is important to seek out ideas that your ideal clients are already interested in. One way to identify great ideas for each category is to perform a Google search to see what topics are already trending online. There are also many keyword tools that can help you identify topics your ideal clients are currently interested in. Later, when we discuss ClientJam in greater detail, we will show you how I.D.E.A.S. 365 provides a starting point with templates for every day of the year so that you can simply import, fill them out with popular topics, and use them to launch your content marketing calendar.

LINKEDIN'S ENGAGEMENT ALGORITHM

So far we've discussed leveraging your *content* on LinkedIn to turn strangers into people who will come to trust you. The other tool at our disposal for expanding your circle of influence is LinkedIn's secret technology: their *algorithm*.

Imagine you post an article on LinkedIn. How many views do you typically get? For most people just starting out, this is not a very large number. No matter how much you try, regardless of the quality of your post, it simply doesn't get shared inside LinkedIn beyond a few people. This is all happening because of a LinkedIn algorithm that decides how far a post will go, which they have lovingly dubbed: *FollowFeed*.

Like any other social media platform, LinkedIn thrives on ENGAGEMENT. They need people to stay engaged so that there are maximum premium users and eyeballs on their advertising. It is therefore in their business interest to have a technology in place that can quickly discover those posts they believe will keep as many eyeballs on the network as possible.

LinkedIn also seeks to keep content quality at a maximum by removing spammy or inappropriate posts as soon as they are created. With millions of posts being created every minute, it is simply impossible to address these requirements without a dedicated algorithm such as FollowFeed.

Here's a brief overview of how it works from one of the graphics LinkedIn provided on their engineering blog[17]:

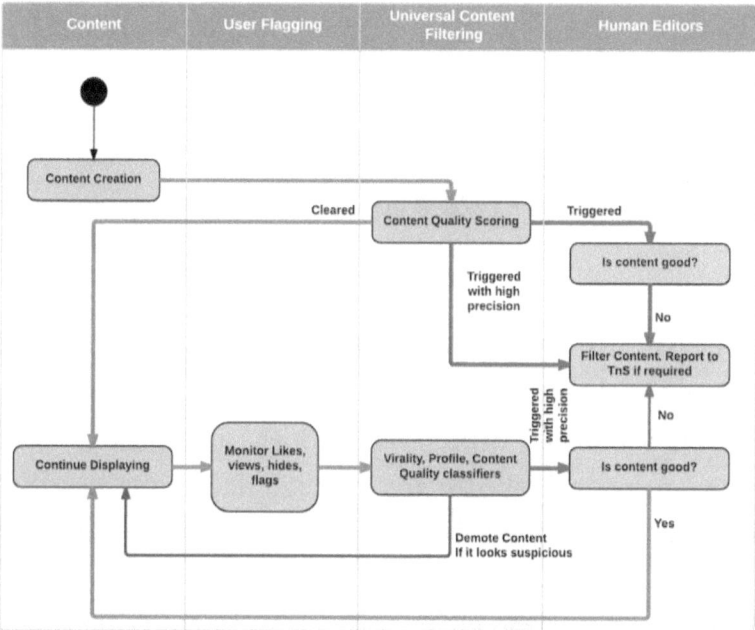

The FollowFeed algorithm was originally developed as a spam-fighting technology, but it has quickly evolved to be the main engine through which decisions about a post are made. The algorithm determines in an instant if a post will go viral or be dead on arrival.

LinkedIn uses what they call a 'Man + Machine' approach. First, an artificial intelligence machine will review your post and grade it based on certain predetermined quality metrics. If your post passes that initial filter, it may go to a human for verification and grading. If everything passes, then your post is shared to larger and larger audiences for engagement over time, each time going through concentric cycles of verification in the Man + Machine algorithm.

While the technical aspects of this may seem daunting, there are a couple of observable rules we've seen through our testing that the algorithm appears to follow to determine the final reach of a post:

*We've found that to be promoted by the LinkedIn algorithm to more people than your closest connections, a post needs to get reactions, comments, and shares from a minimum of **10-15 people** during a **2-hour** period just after the post has been created.*

Let's be clear here; if anyone tells you they know for sure how the LinkedIn algorithm works, they are not telling you the truth. The fact is, many experts—including my team—have run extensive tests on LinkedIn and through deduction, have arrived at estimates like the one I've outlined above. The one thing most people can agree on is this; LinkedIn's free, organic reach has been decreasing as they ramp up and provide more paid offers.

This means that engagement must be addressed intentionally, and thankfully, LinkedIn has provided several tools to increase organic reach:

1. *Hashtags* (to help categorize and share content)
2. *Tags* (to share content with specific people)
3. *Groups* (to help build communities of engagement)
4. *Reactions* (A system of Likes, Comments, and Shares)
5. *Messaging* (for people to share and organize content)

All of these tools are geared toward increasing the engagement of your posts. I like to say that frankly, LinkedIn—like all other social platforms—is an *engagement pod*. However, if because of the rampant misinformation online, someone tells you they don't like engagement pods, you should ask them if they like the social platform in the first place, because engagement is essentially what they all practice. Engagement is the prime directive of social networks.

One can see evidence that engagement is important to LinkedIn, because they once launched a 'pod' of their own called 'Elevate', an employee advocacy product they created for larger corporations. (LinkedIn Elevate is no longer a separate product. As of this writing, it has been morphed into LinkedIn's free Company Pages toolkit). In the third section of this book, we'll discuss further about LinkedIn Elevate and the various options available for increasing the engagement and reach of your posts.

LinkedIn Elevate

Like other social networks, LinkedIn has steadily decreased organic engagement for posts over time. The result is that coordinated engagement strategies are needed which comply and leverage their algorithm, so more people will see your posts.

In a third section of this book, we will discuss how ClientJam uniquely helps you achieve high levels of reach by safely and *ethically* leveraging—and complying with—the LinkedIn algorithm.

CHAPTER 12: ACTION ITEMS

1. Visit your 'My Plan' page on ClientJam.com.

2. Reflect on your thoughts and insights from this chapter and consider how you will use them to continue creating your Social Velocity content marketing plan.

3. In the 'TRUST' section of the REACH tab, describe what strategies you will use to create a level of trust that will attract people to consider your offer.

13. Offer

One of the most pivotal points in a story is the change phase when the hero (your client) meets the guide (you). Think of when young Luke Skywalker met Yoda in *Star Wars*. Or when Jesus met John the Baptist. Or when Mark Zuckerberg met with Steve Jobs for advice and mentorship. Prospects will admit at some point that they need help, and it is our role as the guide to be there for them, ready with great insights and proof that we can help them achieve their goals.

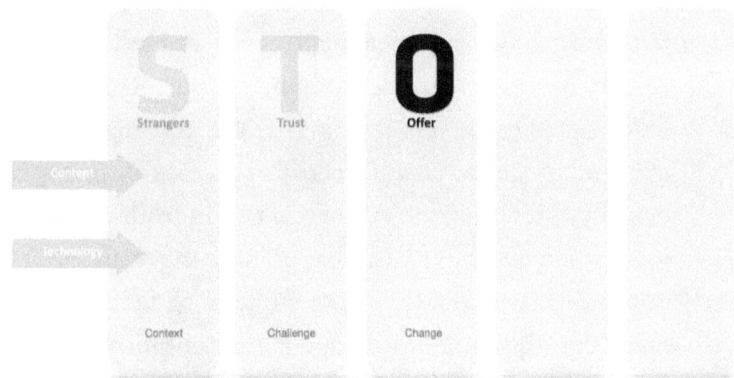

This is the phase when you get to present your OFFER. Your high-value offer can be done in person, over the phone, as an evergreen presentation, or in an online videoconference.

There are three important questions to ask about this phase. First, how will you invite people off of LinkedIn to receive or review your offer? Second, in what format will the meeting take place? Will it be done in person, or delivered as an evergreen webinar or presentation? And third, how will you conduct the meeting itself in order to achieve both your goals and the goals of the prospect?

1. The best way I've seen for getting people off of LinkedIn and into the offer phase is to move them to an email opt-in. Provide a lead magnet, something of value that helps them achieve a portion of their goals in exchange for their email. Once you have their email, you can now nurture the relationship over time. The lead magnet is up to you, but consider it carefully because if it doesn't provide value, you would have made a poor first impression.
2. There are several format options for the offer phase, ranging from free or paid consultations, to evergreen presentations or live webinars. Choose a format that fits your strengths and remember to use the meeting to serve, not sell.
3. Which brings us to the content of the offer meeting itself. Unfortunately, in this meeting phase, too many professionals talk endlessly about *how* they create success for their clients. They talk about features and benefits when in truth the prospect isn't focused on those details at that point in the relationship. Just like in the Strangers phase, where we tend to talk too much about ourselves, this is another huge communication disconnect. We need to talk less about how we will create solutions for our clients because, in the end, this story is not about us. It's about the prospect.

Prospects care more about their current challenges and potential future outcomes when they first meet with you. The features of how you will get them to the Promised Land are secondary. You'll get so much more mileage out of showing you fully understand their current pain and future desired pleasure. Your goals in this phase are to HELP your clients as much as possible, shift their belief systems with deep insights into what they are experiencing, and provide evidence that you can solve their problems.

One of my best experiences in the offer phase was when I met with and became a client of 'Content DNA' author and LinkedIn expert John Espirian, who I now follow and have become good friends with. In our initial consultation meeting, John truly embodied the idea of what he calls *'relentless helpfulness'*. In an interview on my Profitable Happiness Podcast[18], John spoke about his passion for helping others, and how it has become the center of his brand and content marketing strategy. By focusing on helpfulness during the offer phase meeting with me, the client, John created the most powerful impression imaginable, which is why he is still one of my favorite online mentors.

Instead of listing off your various service features and benefits, the offer phase is a great opportunity to unearth a prospect's emotions, offer your help, and bring them to a place of understanding that you are an irreplaceable resource for them.

Another mentor of mine who comes to mind with respect to being relentlessly helpful is Neil Patel, whom I also interviewed on the Profitable Happiness Podcast[19].

As a result of his helpfulness, Neil Patel is regarded as perhaps the world's top digital marketing expert. If you type the following words in an online search—*Top Online Marketing Experts*—you will most probably see his name show up on page one, usually as number one!

His blog articles and videos are in-depth, extremely well-researched, and widely shared online. They are also the entry level into his Offer phase. At the end of each article is a clearly stated Call To Action. And after the amount of value he provides, it is difficult not to take him up on his offer to move further into his funnel.

Neil Patel likes to say, "Behind every successful person are a lot of unsuccessful years." However, based on what I've seen him do over the years, he could easily restate that to, "Behind every successful person are a lot of years of helping others!"

BUILDING YOUR S.T.O.R.Y. FUNNEL

Since we're now halfway through describing the S.T.O.R.Y. funnel, let's take a look at how we leverage LinkedIn to see your funnel in action.

Dr. Pelè

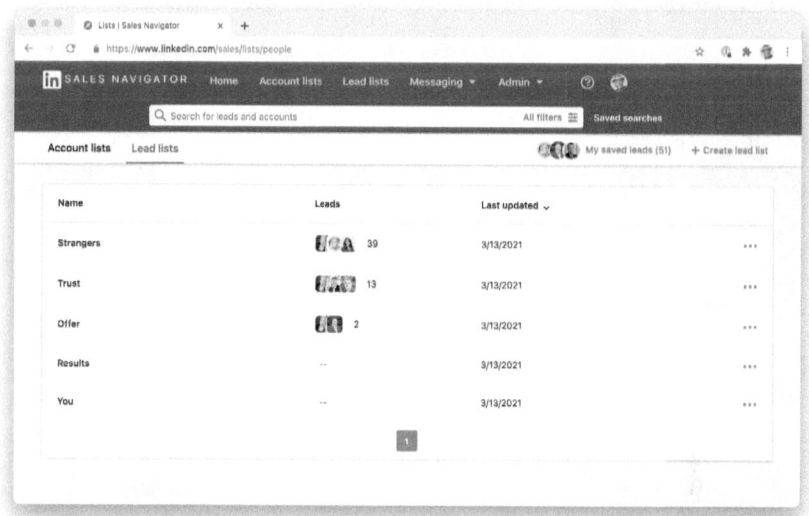

This diagram shows LinkedIn's Sales Navigator, which is their premium software for helping you find and grow relationships on LinkedIn. While it has a limited feature set, it can be used as a simple CRM (customer relationship management) tool to manage the flow of prospects through your S.T.O.R.Y. funnel.

As you can see from the diagram, we have created Lead lists representing each phase of the S.T.O.R.Y. funnel. You can see that in the timeframe captured, 39 people were sent invitations to connect based on content engagement, event participation, or some other criteria, determined in the *manual* process of sharing your content weekly. (Remember, we NEVER use automation, bots, or browser plugins!)

You can also see that 13 people have moved from the Strangers phase to the Trust phase, which means they have come into our community as 1st-degree connections and will now see our content more readily.

Finally, you can see that 2 people have accepted our invitation and moved into the Offer phase, meaning that they are now ready to receive a presentation or high-proximity interaction with us. Here is a detailed look at how you can move each user through the funnel.

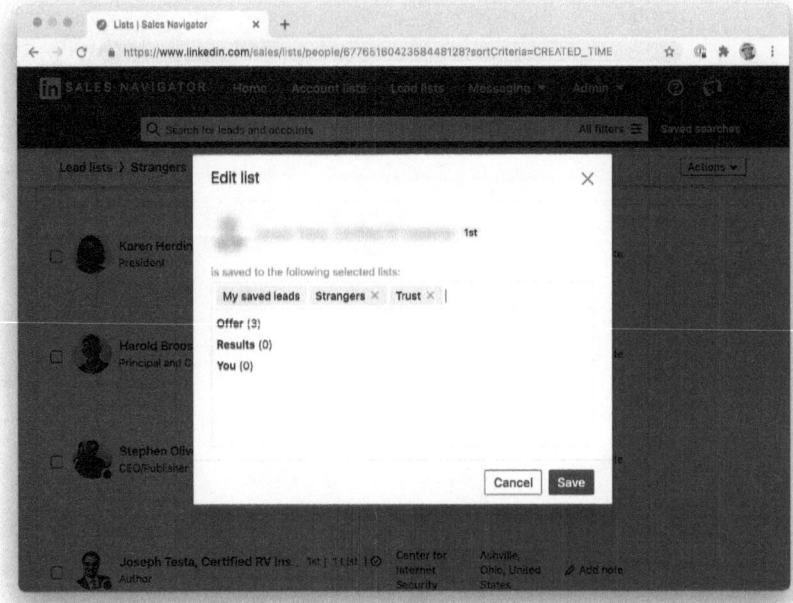

By having visual access to how people are moving through your funnel inside LinkedIn, you are able to make decisions about who to reach out to and when. Without this kind of visibility, nurturing leads on LinkedIn can be like taking a walk with blindfolds on. It's important to see how people are responding to your content and efforts to move them through your funnel.

Let's now take a look at our final two content marketing plan phases, which we call the 'Results' and 'You' parts of the S.T.O.R.Y. funnel. What's interesting about these final two phases is that they are not traditionally seen as business development areas. But in truth, they are the most powerful forms of business development available to us.

CHAPTER 13: ACTION ITEMS

1. Visit your 'My Plan' page on ClientJam.com.

2. Reflect on your thoughts and insights from this chapter and consider how you will use them to continue creating your Social Velocity content marketing plan.

3. In the 'OFFER' section of the REACH tab, describe your presentation plan for converting prospects into clients.

14. Results

Please take a seat, tap yourself on the back five times, and shout "Yeah!" You've done a fantastic job. You've taken a complete stranger from LinkedIn or wherever they first met you and turned them into a high-value client! You helped them get to know you by using *content* to position yourself as an authority in your specific niche, and you earned their trust slowly but surely over time. You met with them, provided your offer, listened to their concerns, and finally, they signed on to work with you. Again, please tap yourself on the back. Congratulations!

But you may ask: If we've generated a lead and converted them into a client, why isn't this the end of the process? Why must we continue to leverage the power of S.T.O.R.Y. after a prospect has already become a client?

Here's why: your very best lead generation tool is word-of-mouth referrals, and you can only get those by delivering excellent results to your existing clients and launching an intentional, measurable referral system.

Now, that may sound simple, but it isn't. The trick to getting results for clients and having them form the opinion that you are someone they should refer lies in great *leadership*. Just as most consultants, advisors, and coaches didn't sign up to become sales and marketing experts when they started on their career journeys, they probably also didn't realize that they would have to become 'leaders' for their clients.

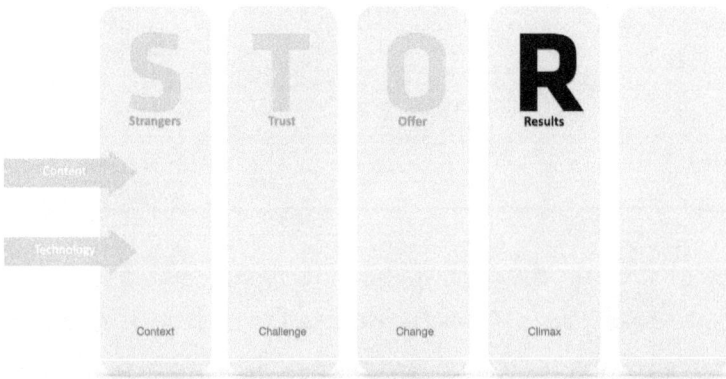

You would be correct if you believe that many coaches, advisors, and consultants wouldn't even consider the Results phase—when they're delivering results for a client—to be part of a lead generation strategy per se. However, I believe that to be a mistake. Client referrals are the easiest prospects to close and should ideally represent a solid percentage of your lead generation strategy. The results phase is an incredibly important part of your lead generation process because it's where you get to earn the right to be referred to future high-value clients.

ONE STORY ENDS, ANOTHER BEGINS

After the context, challenge, and change phases of a story, we have the climax. The climax is that point in a story when the reward is finally visible to the hero just across the horizon. The hero's initial journey starts to look like it is coming to an end. The hero has seized the sword and is ready to strike the dragon but must be proven worthy or else, the battle, and life itself will be lost. A new story gap is opened, and we are back to wondering what will happen next!

The Results phase is where you must prove to your client that you are worthy of the trust they initially placed in you and that you are worthy of being referred by them to future high-value clients. You may not have a 100% guarantee that you will succeed with a client (since their execution of strategy is part of the equation), but your chances are much better if you put your relationship with them in the context of an eventual referral right from the start. This is where you must become the leader who takes your followers to the Promised Land. Together, you and your client must slay the dragon—or else the kingdom will be lost!

EXCELLENCE STARTS ON THE INSIDE

Far too many consultants, advisors, and coaches treat the Results phase as though they've forgotten that their reputation from current and past clients will precede them. This is why we see a lot of very aggressive online marketing for products and services that, in the end, really aren't very good on the inside.

Steve Jobs is celebrated for the beautiful Apple products that people can see, hear, and touch. What is not so well known was his commitment to creating beauty on the inside of his products, where no one could ever see.

According to Walter Isaacson, his biographer, he learned this design philosophy from his father, Paul. In a *60 Minutes*[20] episode, Isaacson described how Paul Jobs would ask the young Steve to help him build fences around their home in Mountain View California. One day, while they were at work, Paul shared some advice with his son:

"You've got to make the back of the fence, that nobody will see, just as good-looking as the front of the fence. Even though nobody will see it, you will know, and that will show that you're dedicated to making something perfect."

This advice stuck with Steve Jobs, and he used it to build a company that seeks excellence everywhere, starting from the inside, where no one can see.

If we want to create world-class products and services, we should borrow a leaf from Steve Jobs and Apple. We should work hard to ignore all the get-rich-quick and sizzle-with-no-steak strategies people offer online, and actually build great products and services on the inside. Our clients will experience this greatness on the inside and turn around and tell the world all about it.

Beware, for the reverse is also true. If we continue to be great at bringing in new clients, only to leave them feeling unsupported on the inside, the market will hear about that as well, and our lead generation will eventually grind to a halt because of our bad reputation.

DELIVER WHAT YOU PROMISE

I remember once attending an online course where I paid $10,000 upfront. The hype for this course on the Internet was simply amazing! Every day I received emails and advertisements until I finally acquiesced. But once I got inside the service, there was absolutely no support. I was essentially on my own. No one was willing to spend any one-on-one time with me—even for a fee—and no one had any answers for me other than "Go watch the videos." I can tell you it was one of the most annoying experiences of my professional life. The guru who sold the course to me on all those online advertisements was nowhere to be found! Spending that much money and getting to only watch videos of him in a membership area was an insult I couldn't bear.

This got me thinking about an important paradox. What we (as coaches, advisors, and consultants) sell on the outside may well need to be about the external goals the client thinks they want to achieve. However, once they arrive on the inside, we have to provide them with the tools that will help them achieve their goals—whether they know it or not. On the outside, we may have to sell the promise of tangible results, but on the inside, we must provide learning and support based on realities such as mindset and execution.

The key to inspiring the right mindset and supporting execution is leadership. When done right, your leadership will be that rare quality that allows your clients to work well with you and perform at their very best. Being a leader for your clients helps you deliver on what you promised. The service-provider-as-influential-leader approach is the best way I've seen to influence clients toward both internal clarity and external results.

YOUR REFERRAL MAGNET

In the Results phase, you've been focused on helping your clients get results. Additionally, your end goal has always been the side effect of referrals. Happy clients will refer if they are asked to. (By the way, you will learn in the next section that clients won't necessarily refer you just for doing a good job. You have to proactively *ask* for referrals!)

What we need to do is create a referral package that, once they are exposed to it, will draw their network in to consider your offer. This means that we have to pull together onto a sales page on your website an opt-in package that will pre-sell anyone your clients refer you to.

This package could be the same presentation you created for the Offer phase. It could be a webinar, a video, a series of client case studies, or testimonials. It must contain social proof and a call to action. The key is to have at the ready an easy-to-share link that you can provide to your clients at the moment when they appear to be getting results, and not a moment before or after! This is the point at which they are most motivated to support you and refer you.

Think of a Referral Magnet as a social-proof-heavy form of a lead magnet, except that it is a 'warm' presentation because you are introduced by an existing, happy client. Make sure that you do all the work for your client. Don't leave anything to chance or to the client. They are busy. Find the people they need to send your Referral Magnet to, create the sales landing page for it, and simply provide your clients a sharable link.

Remember, your existing clients can be your best sales force! Make sure to provide them with the leads and referral magnets they need to introduce you to others. And make it as easy as clicking a button!

As we've done in each step so far, consider what your leadership style is. Brainstorm specific strategies and tactics you might use to help your clients get results. Write them down in your ClientJam Content Marketing Plan.

Dr. Pelè

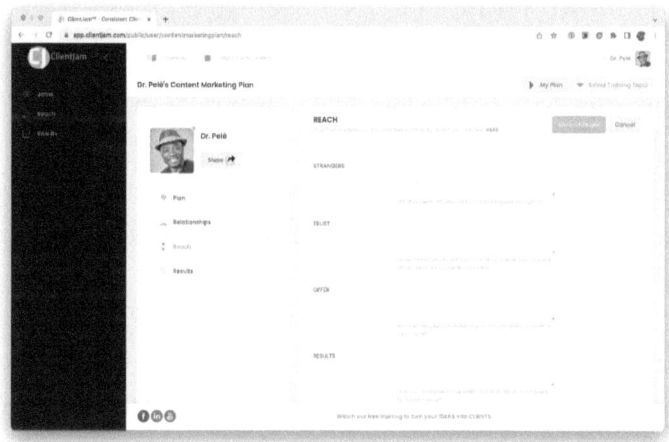

Even though it might seem that creating client results is outside of a traditional business development scope, it is in many ways the most important thing you can do to make your future business development easier. In the next—'You'—phase of the S.T.O.R.Y. funnel, we will discuss how you can go about collecting the powerful client stories and referrals that will bring in future business on autopilot.

CHAPTER 14: ACTION ITEMS

1. Visit your 'My Plan' page on ClientJam.com.

2. Reflect on your thoughts and insights from this chapter and consider how you will use them to continue creating your Social Velocity content marketing plan.

3. In the 'RESULTS' section of the REACH tab, describe how you will convert your existing clients into lead magnets for future clients.

15. You

Every great story ends with a moral. We learn something from a story that changes our lives for the better. Every parable has a point. We tell the parable in anticipation of the point we're going to make. This is exactly how the story of your client's journey to success with you should conclude. Your client had a challenge, met you, you introduced change into their life, and from that change, a climax of success was created. Now it's time to learn the moral of the story. This is where the client gets a chance to tell the story of YOU that can help you convert future clients. I call this the *conversion* phase of your S.T.O.R.Y. funnel.

The YOU phase is the point in time when all successes have been achieved, and now we want to know what it all means so we can convert it into future success. What did we learn? Why did we go through all the trials and tribulations? What was the meaning of the story?

WHEN CLIENTS TELL GREAT STORIES ABOUT YOU

The final stage of a high-value client's S.T.O.R.Y. funnel is YOU. This is the stage where your client has had an opportunity to find you, work with you, evaluate the work they've done with you, and decide for themselves what it all means. The best moral of the story that can come out of this phase is that you are worthy of being referred to others.

If we can correctly execute the referral of you in this phase of your relationship with clients, you will be able to attract all the high-value clients you want going forward. When your clients tell others how great you are, you will be unstoppable! That's how powerful this final phase can be. According to *The New York Times*, a whopping 65% of all new business in the United States comes from referrals.[12] That's an amazing percentage and it goes to show the outstanding power of trust that gets transferred from one person to another.

Word-of-mouth referrals are important. In fact, according to Nielsen's Global Trust in Advertising and Brand Messages[21], the most trust (92%) is found in "recommendations from people I know." In sharp contrast, the same report shows that advertising on social networks is only 36% trusted.

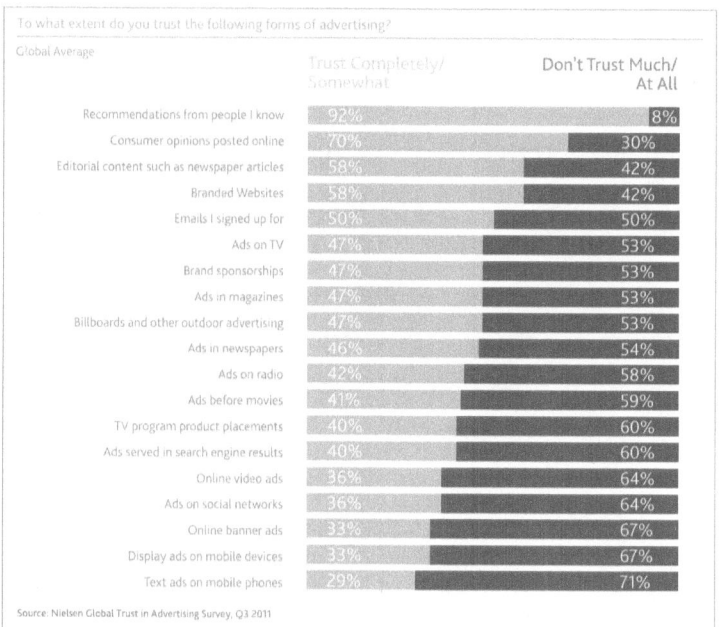

Without a doubt, referrals have been proven to be the most effective means of acquiring high-value clients. Yet, according to John Jantsch in *The Referral Engine*[22], almost 80% of those who say referrals account for over 50% of their business, also readily admit that they have *no* system of any kind for generating referrals. This is why it's so important to call out this phase in your S.T.O.R.Y. funnel. Your goal should be to intentionally, proactively, and consistently help your clients refer you to others.

WHY REFERRALS SEEM SO HARD TO GET

Difficulties with getting referrals usually come from three misconceptions and wrong beliefs about them: *Results, Rejection,* and *Relying*.

The Hope that RESULTS are enough

Many people believe that if they create great results for clients, they will naturally get referred by them. This couldn't be further from the truth. Clients, in all honesty, are most concerned with "what have you done for me lately?" Out of sight can be truly out of mind. What you did last year for your clients is not necessarily going to be present in their memory this year. The result is that they have no strong reason to refer you that is top of mind and on their radar. You cannot hope that a client will refer you to others because you got them great results. If you do that, you might be waiting for quite a long time. You must *ask* for a referral when the iron is hot!

The Fear of REJECTION from clients

Another difficulty with referrals is asking for them in the first place. There is this huge fear around getting a rejection, just like in any sales call. Admittedly, there is an inherent risk in referring others because you're attaching yourself and your brand to the success (or failure) of the person you're referring. This puts a lot of sales pressure on the process of asking for referrals. In short, because of the fear of rejection, asking for referrals can be even more fearsome than a traditional sales call with a new client.

The Problem with RELYING on clients

The third difficulty with getting referrals is that we rely on our clients to do all the heavy lifting for us. We ask that they find the right prospects, send them the right information, and deliver qualified, interested leads to us. That's an entire lead-generation job we're asking them to perform! No wonder such requests usually go unheeded. If you want this process to work, you have to make it easy on your referral partners or clients. You have to rely on them as little as possible. You should package up your offer and value proposition information in a simple, powerful, and compelling way that is *easy* for your existing clients to share.

THE 4-P REFERRAL PROCESS

The best way to guarantee a consistent stream of referred prospects is to *have* a system for getting referred. Your process is essentially one of doing the prospecting for the client and writing the story of YOU for them to share.

As we discussed earlier, every story has five phases: context, challenge, change, climax, and conversion. All you have to do is write your story using that format and provide it to your clients and referral partners. That way, all they need to do is forward a link to a qualified prospect. Here are the 4-Ps for building a consistent referral system:

1. *Preparation*

First identify four groups of people: influencers, your ideal clients, your ideal referral partners (who have a built-in interest to refer you), and existing clients with whom you have achieved great rapport and results. You must become comfortable with asking for referrals, especially at points in your relationships with referral partners or existing clients where there is a sense that there is a win-win built-in to any referral.

2. Packaging

Once you've identified all the stakeholders in your referral program, you need to equip them with an easily sharable 'referral magnet' package that tells your entire story. Your referral magnets should be educational, valuable, and entertaining, but never 'salesy'.

Ask your existing clients to record a testimonial video to include in the package that you are going to ask them to send to their network. You will get much better results and response rates when your clients' networks can hear it directly from them.

3. Prospecting

The next thing you need is to do the actual prospecting for your referral partners. Don't expect or hope that they will go and find potential prospects for you. Simply hand them a list and help them share your package easily. Make sure that you have a method of measuring the effectiveness of your referral campaigns. As usual, what doesn't get measured can't be improved.

4. Pay for it

Sometimes you have to physically pay your clients as affiliates when they refer you. This is not out of the ordinary. Most companies have referral programs that include a direct financial benefit for making referrals. For example, you could offer a 30% or even a 50% affiliate commission for every referral that turns into a sale. It's quite normal to have referral partnerships that involve remuneration. Whether you are paying with cash or in-kind, make sure that the referral process has built-in reciprocity and win-win.

ASK, AND MAKE IT EASY

The most important point to remember about the 'YOU' phase in your client's story is that even though this is their chance to tell *your* story, you shouldn't ever expect them to take the initiative and do it for you. You must *ask* them, and you must make sharing your story easy for them to do.

A great time to ask for a video testimonial is during or immediately after any interaction where you have demonstrated your value. When your client has achieved a great result, ask for a referral. When your referral partner first says "yes" to a cooperation agreement with you, ask for a referral. The bottom line? *Just ask*!

CHAPTER 15: ACTION ITEMS

1. Visit your 'My Plan' page on ClientJam.com.

2. Reflect on your thoughts and insights from this chapter and consider how you will use them to continue creating your Social Velocity content marketing plan.

3. In the 'YOU' section of the REACH tab, describe how you will collect and share testimonials from your high-value clients.

Dr. Pelè

16. Principle Three: RESULTS

There has perhaps never been a better time for business-to-business coaches, consultants, entrepreneurs, and companies to create *Social Velocity* through content marketing. With close to 740 million users on LinkedIn, and only 3 million posting regularly, this is the most powerful opportunity to expand your RESULTS on social media.

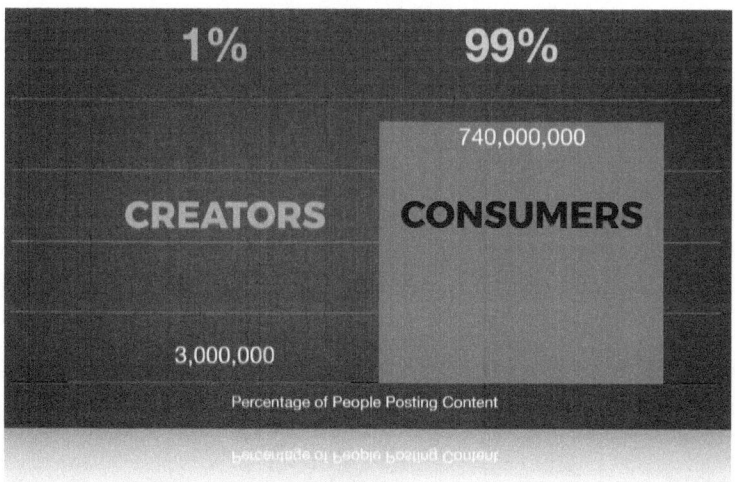

I like to tell my three children, "Creators shape the world. You must strive to be a creator, not merely a consumer." This couldn't be truer on LinkedIn. Some people are fine with merely *consuming* the creations of others. However, it is *creators* who become the Apples and Teslas of the world. With such little competition at the time of this writing, anyone posting regularly—as a content creator—stands an excellent chance of getting Social Velocity and growing a sizable following.

However, as we've discussed earlier, there is a challenge. Even though the opportunity is great, bad content quality will not get social reach. No one can easily game a social platform's algorithm, and even if you tried, the platform would catch on quickly. The only thing that gets great reach is great content. We, therefore, have to know what's working versus what's not working to slowly but steadily improve our content marketing over time.

The key to improving your content lies in *analytics*. When management expert Peter Drucker famously said, "If you can't measure it, you can't improve it," he was referring to the power of quantification through analytics. Analytics allow you to see what's working and what's not working so that you can make intelligent, timely decisions about how to improve your content performance, and therefore, your results.

LinkedIn has all the data you would ever need to understand how your content is working—or not working—with your target audience. However, it is not organized and arranged in such a manner as to be meaningful to you. If, as an individual, you wanted to answer a simple question like, "what are my most effective types of posts?" you would have to scroll through weeks and perhaps months of feed posts and keep detailed spreadsheets just to get a little bit of a useful answer. (In all fairness, LinkedIn does provide some post analytics, but it is—at the time of this writing—only for Company Pages). If you're a coach, consultant, or entrepreneur, you should ideally be posting as a person—yourself—because people build relationships and do business with people, not companies.

ClientJam allows you—posting as a person—to track how many people clicked on your post links and puts it all into meaningful visuals and tables so that you can make sense of your data and take appropriate action.

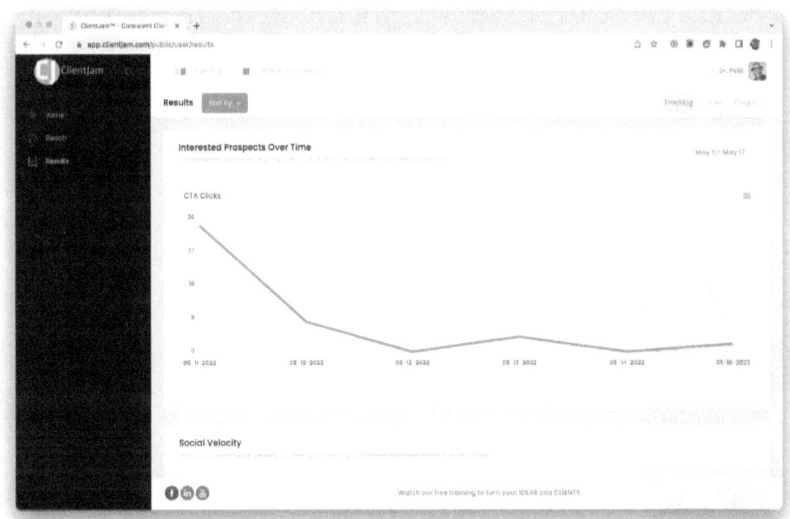

Here are the ways we calculate the two most important requirements for knowing what's working and what's not: Social Velocity, and Engagement. First, let's look at how we measure your results for Social Velocity:

Social Velocity = (Reactions x 1) +
(Comments x 2) +
(Clicks x 3)

The reason we provide different weights to these three *interaction* attributes is because we believe that, as a measure of your ideal client's true feelings about your content, *reactions* have some value, but not as much as *comments*. It takes more connection with you and your content for someone to publicly provide a comment.

As such we score reactions as a '1' and comments as a '2'. Similarly, we believe that when someone *clicks* on a link you've provided to go back to your website, they've demonstrated the ultimate level of connection with your content, so we score that a '3'.

Engagement is calculated as a percentage measure of how many people chose to *interact* with your content after viewing it:

Engagement = (Social Velocity ÷ Views) x 100%

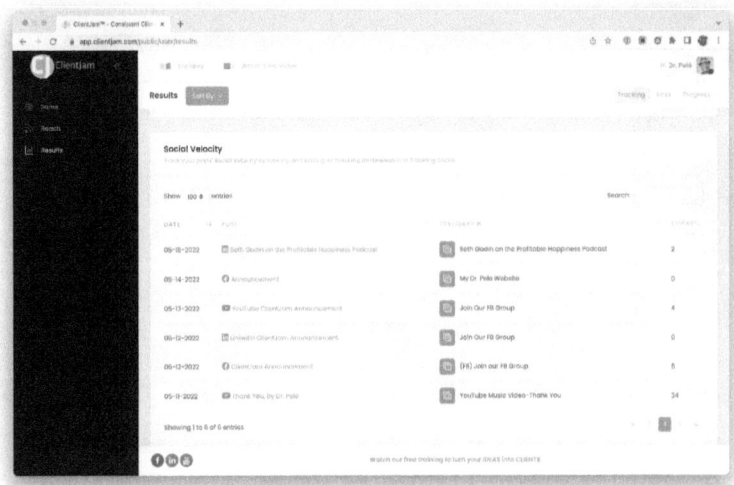

By seeing these data points over time, we will know exactly what to do to serve our audience. Analytics, therefore, becomes so much more than just pretty graphs and tables about reactions, comments, and views for each post. It becomes our *language* for improving content, which is literally how we will survive and thrive, just like the honeybee in one of my favorite analogies from nature.

THE DANCE OF THE HONEYBEE

One of the most remarkable and fascinating phenomena in nature is the dance of the honeybee. Affectionately called the 'waggle dance' by beekeepers, the dance is an ingenious method of communication used by honeybees to indicate the precise direction and distance of a newly discovered food source. In an interesting twist of nature's vast propensity for magical, inexplicable intelligence, the honeybee can communicate *Social Velocity* for the survival of the hive!

Here's how it works. Every day, thousands of honeybees leave their hives in search of nectar, their food source provided by flowers. When one of them discovers nectar at a specific location, it will fly back to the hive, retaining that location in memory. Once it is back at the hive, the bee will 'dance' in a very specific pattern, which, like a language, accurately informs the other bees about the direction and distance of the food source.

By dancing in a specific *direction* relative to the sun and their hive, the bee communicates the direction of the food source. And by dancing for a specific duration of time, it communicates the *distance* of the food source.

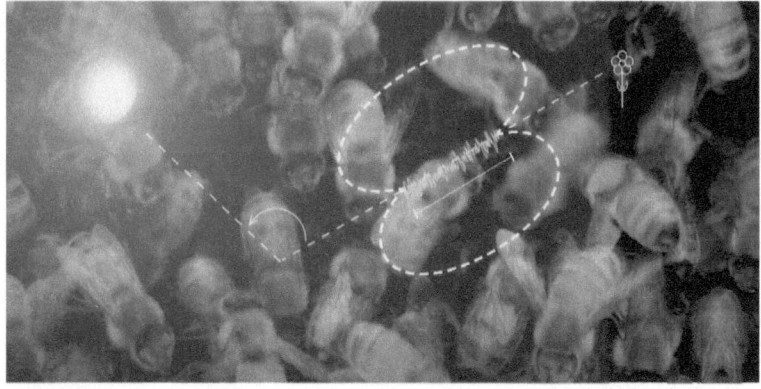

Once the other bees understand the dance, they follow what they've learned back to the newly discovered food source, bring back the good nectar, and perpetuate their survival.

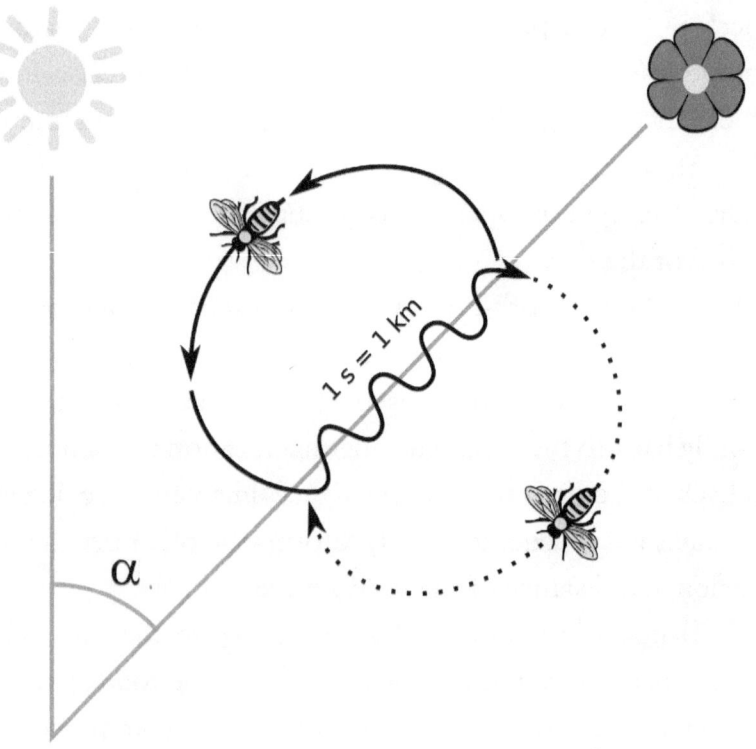

This beautiful and sophisticated waggle dance of the honeybee is actually a highly developed survival mechanism. If the bees do not accurately communicate their descriptions of distance and direction—which we would call *Social Velocity*—their colony will not survive.

In the same way, if we continue to create content on social media, but get no feedback about it, no measurements, no analytics telling us what is working or not working, we will not be able to improve our business results.

Remember when we talked earlier about Apple's success being attributed to their Big Data and behavioral economics feedback from customers? Well, their data was doing a waggle dance!

We need to send out content that will bring us back graphs, tables, and data to answer our questions about what's working and what's not. If we can't see this data, it would be like trying to drive a car blindfolded. We would crash. Without analytics, we would never know where our best content is. And we would never know how to continue delivering what our audience wants. In short, if we can't get good information about the direction and distance of our content, just like the bees, we simply won't survive with content marketing as a business development strategy.

THE WAGGLE ANALYTICS STRATEGY

In this section, we're going to walk through an imaginary, but specific example of how you might use results analytics to build relationships and increase the reach of your content.

Imagine that you've committed to posting content two or three times a week for a month. Let's also imagine that you've chosen to post with four different types of content: video, text, graphics, and polls. Doing this over a month would give you ample data if you could see it all in one place, which is the hard part because the data is scattered everywhere on LinkedIn. Let's take a look at a simple strategy for improving your content marketing based on measurements. I call it the Waggle Content Strategy.

Remember we talked about how honeybees venture out, find good food, and bring back the news of it to the hive as a waggle dance? Well, that's what your content should do for you. Your posts are your emissaries, going out into the LinkedIn world and coming back to do an analytics 'dance' that will help you discover what works and what doesn't for your ideal audience.

However, before you launch a waggle strategy, you have to make sure you're not casting too wide of a net. Based on some of the foundational things we've already covered, here are some things to consider:

1. Identify very clearly whom you serve
2. Keep connections that will resonate with your content
3. Unfollow those who wouldn't care about your content
4. Serve with your content, don't sell
5. Grow trust through consistency, show up!
6. Focus on your buyer, not yourself, the seller
7. Be relentlessly HELPFUL with your content
8. Have calls to action in some of your content

Once you have these things in place, you're ready to sit back and watch your content dance for you and tell you where the food is! Here now is a non-comprehensive, typical set of specific questions that analytics can help you answer from your month of activity:

- What types of posts are resonating the most with my ideal audience? (Text, video, polls, graphics, etc.).
- What specific, micro-problems do my ideal clients have that I need to be solving?
- Which posts of mine are getting the most Social Velocity and Engagement?
- If my engagement is low, could it be that the people viewing my data are perhaps NOT my ideal clients? Could it be that

I have too many connections with people that wouldn't even care about my content?
- If my velocity is low, what can I do to get more reactions and comments from my ideal clients? Should I perhaps ask more questions, provide more levity, more edutainment? What's really working, and what's not?

Watching your data each week, you will begin to see some patterns. You will start to notice how your ideal clients are responding (or not responding) to your content. You will be able to determine why certain posts are effective and others not so much. You may find that you need to take action to reduce the number of connections you have (or people you're following) to keep only those who might care about your data. With the insights you gain from your data, you will be able to pivot as needed or proceed with your best foot forward.

As you watch your content over time, you will need to continuously review and monitor your data on several metrics points, which I call 'C.O.U.N.T.'

- Conversions
- Opportunities
- Uniques
- Numbers
- Traffic

By 'counting' these five metrics frameworks, you are effectively watching the waggle dance of your content 'honeybees'. By monitoring these metrics, you are on a path to improve your content, build relationships, and land more ideal, high-value clients. Let's look at each metric in more detail.

17. Conversions

Perhaps the single most important question you want answered about your content is whether or not it is driving any lead conversions. At the end of the day, you're not posting on LinkedIn and engaging with others purely for fun. Content marketing is not a 'tick the box' activity. Its value is ultimately to feed your sales engine and produce measurable new-client results. The way to stay on top of how well you're doing in this area is by measuring your *conversions*.

Take a look at the trends in your S.T.O.R.Y. funnel. Are you seeing daily or weekly movement from stage to stage? If not, why not? What could you alter in your LinkedIn profile, or your post content, that would help to improve your lead conversions?

Another strategy might be to look at the *quality* of the leads you're converting. Are your leads taking actions that get them off of LinkedIn, and back to your website? Once they are on your website, are they downloading anything, opting in, or registering for anything?

Finally, take a look at each stage of your funnel and answer questions directly related to them. For example, you might want to know how many Strangers you've invited to join you in the Trust area (as connections) have actually accepted your invitation. How many are rejecting your invitation, and what patterns can you deduce to answer the question of why they are not connecting with you? By answering these questions, you develop conversion rates at every stage of your story funnel. And it is these conversion rates that tell you whether your content marketing strategy is working, or not.

Similarly, in the Trust phase, you can inquire from your funnel numbers whether there is a positive or negative trend in people accepting your invitation for a closer proximity interaction.

Understanding your lead conversion rates at each stage of your S.T.O.R.Y. funnel will help you take the necessary actions to ensure that your most qualified prospects are moving steadily through your pipeline.

CHAPTER 17: ACTION ITEMS

1. Visit your 'My Plan' page on ClientJam.com.

2. Reflect on your thoughts and insights from this chapter and consider how you will use them to continue creating your Social Velocity content marketing plan.

3. In the 'CONVERSIONS' section of the RESULTS tab, describe your plan for converting content marketing prospects into high-value clients.

18. Opportunities

Another important question approach is to ask what *opportunities* you might be discovering, or missing, based on reviewing your analytics. For example, which of your posts may have high views, but low engagement, and why? Or perhaps you could look for gaps, such as where you might be dropping leads in your S.T.O.R.Y. funnel. Where are the bottlenecks, and where is the best performance overall?

You might also want to know what type of posts are most successful for you. Are your articles getting better traction than your posts? Are your videos being shared more than your text posts? Are you getting great responses in your polls? All of these questions will help you to unearth potential opportunities in your content marketing that may not be readily visible until you dig through your data over time.

Based on the strengths and opportunities you discover from your data, you can now begin to consider how you can best optimize your content marketing to more completely meet your sales and business goals.

CHAPTER 18: ACTION ITEMS

1. Visit your 'My Plan' page on ClientJam.com.

2. Reflect on your thoughts and insights from this chapter and consider how you will use them to continue creating your Social Velocity content marketing plan.

3. In the 'OPPORTUNITIES' section of the RESULTS tab, describe what opportunities you hope to uncover and discover as a result of measuring your content performance.

19. Uniques

The next set of questions you want your waggling content to answer for you is central to the growth and health of your circle of influence. You want to know over time if you are growing your tribe. To fully gain clarity on this class of data, some metrics you could look into are the number of *unique* (new) followers you've been acquiring over time.

If that number is increasing, then your tribe is growing. However, what is not so obvious is when you compare those following you versus those whom you follow. LinkedIn allows a maximum of 30,000 connections. Also, every connection is a follower. So, when you look at your data, if the number of people you follow is close to or equivalent to the number who follow you, then you can quickly deduce that perhaps your followers are only there because they are connected to you. This means they weren't necessarily voluntary participants that joined your follower list as a result of your content. A healthy content marketing strategy should produce a follower list that is greater than those you are following.

Social Velocity

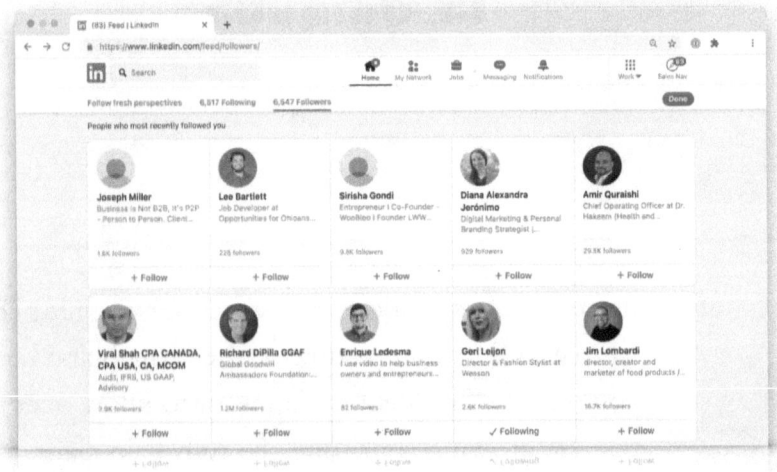

Another area to look at is those who are viewing your profile. This particular metric is so important that LinkedIn actually has really good data for it. By simply clicking the 'Who Viewed Your Profile' link, you can see a graph and detailed information about who is viewing your profile. This is a great indicator of the effectiveness of your profile and content efforts.

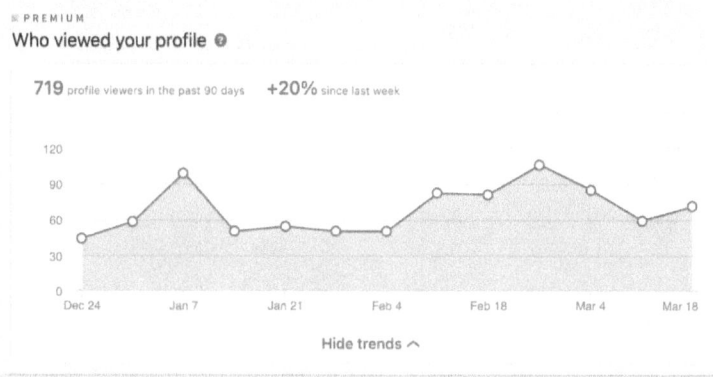

Those who viewed your profile might be good candidates to initiate direct conversations with. You may even want to connect with them if they are not already 1st-degree connections. In the end, the number of unique visitors you're having will give you a good sense of how your content marketing is working, (or not working).

CHAPTER 20: ACTION ITEMS

1. Visit your 'My Plan' page on ClientJam.com.

2. Reflect on your thoughts and insights from this chapter and consider how you will use them to continue creating your Social Velocity content marketing plan.

3. In the 'UNIQUES' section of the RESULTS tab, forecast how many unique (new) followers you hope to attract each month.

20. Numbers

The next area of information you should be tracking are your *leading and lagging* measures. Lagging Indicators are backward-looking. They tell you whether or not you have achieved a specific goal or not. The most obvious examples would be sales figures or qualified leads. Certainly, leads and sales outcomes are the ultimate goals of any business, but you should also be looking at the less tangible business goals that can give you a sense of your likelihood to achieve your final outcome goals.

These are called Leading Indicators, and they are numbers about something in your business that tells you if you are likely to achieve an outcome or goal. For example, if you have many speaking invitations showing up in your calendar, that might tell you that you will end up with new coaching clients in a certain year.

Other Leading Indicators are your Social Velocity and Engagement calculations we've discussed previously, as well as how many clicks you're seeing to your website or landing page offer.

All of these numbers should be tied to your business goals, both tangible, and intangible, both leading, and lagging.

CHAPTER 20: ACTION ITEMS

1. Visit your 'My Plan' page on ClientJam.com.

2. Reflect on your thoughts and insights from this chapter and consider how you will use them to continue creating your Social Velocity content marketing plan.

3. In the 'NUMBERS' section of the RESULTS tab, describe the leading and lagging indicators you will measure to gauge the progress of your content marketing along the way.

21. Traffic

This class of numbers is all about getting people OFF of LinkedIn and onto your website or opt-in landing pages. At the end of the day, we all have to accept that we do not own LinkedIn (understatement of the century, perhaps?) If LinkedIn decides to change policies or do something that endangers the presence of your connections, what options do you have? Not much. What you can do is make sure that you provide options for people interested in your work to join you in an email list, separate community, or even in your personal Rolodex or contact list. Getting people to join you outside of LinkedIn is perhaps one of the most important kinds of traffic you can measure.

You should also make sure that you're measuring the results you're creating for clients and the testimonials they are giving you as a result of your success with them. Remember, the business development process (and therefore counting) should not end once you get a customer. It never really stops because you need to know how well you're doing in getting your customers to actively refer you and tell others the wonderful story of you.

PUTTING IT ALL TOGETHER

Once you are able to use content to build relationships, expand your reach, and measure your results, you will have fully arrived at Social Velocity. In the next section, we will go into specific details about how you can use ClientJam to land your highest-value clients with content marketing on LinkedIn.

CHAPTER 21: ACTION ITEMS

1. Visit your 'My Plan' page on ClientJam.com.

2. Reflect on your thoughts and insights from this chapter and consider how you will use them to continue creating your Social Velocity content marketing plan.

3. In the 'TRAFFIC' section of the RESULTS tab, describe what traffic sources you will be measuring and how you will determine their effectiveness along the way?

Dr. Pelè

SECTION 3:
LAUNCHING YOUR CLIENTJAM

Social Velocity

22. Let's Talk About You

Your prospects are exposed to anywhere from 6,000 to 10,000 advertising messages every single day. According to research from Yankelovich[23], 65% of your prospects feel constantly bombarded with too much marketing and advertising. They are gobsmacked with ads, brand logos, videos, images, stories, and endless chatter on social media and even in their email inboxes. The social noise thrown at your prospects has gotten so bad, they've simply tuned out. They are no longer responding.

You, on the other hand, are an expert in your field. You have excelled in both the theory and practice of making solutions for your ideal clients, but you recognize now the huge chasm between making and *marketing*. Right now, you're struggling with how to get seen and heard online so you can develop consistent business from social media.

You're also seeing far too much confusing training online and frankly, you're too busy to focus on marketing, which is becoming more and more like a full-time job. To make matters worse, you are struggling not only with the occasional bout of imposter syndrome we all experience but also with what I call the obscurity dilemma; no one *knows* you! When you signed up to be the excellent coach, consultant, entrepreneur, or business leader you are, no one told you about the obscurity dilemma you'd face in the marketplace. No one told you that you were signing up to become a full-time marketer and salesperson.

So, what do you do?

What do you do to get multiple high-proximity meetings with your ideal, high-value prospects each month? How do you get known? What do you do to get seen and heard by your ideal clients above today's social media crowd? And what can you do to ensure that your content marketing continues to improve in effectiveness to the point where you're surgically and precisely sharing the right information with the right prospects at the right time?

Your answer lies in building a system that will get you off of today's speed-based, hustle-focused, marketing hamster wheels. Your answer lies in *your* behavior change, in focusing on a slower but steadier *ethical* system that works like an asset, continuing to deliver value to your ideal clients over time, long after you've launched it. Your answer lies in building Social Velocity in your marketplace through the power of content.

"But Dr. Pelè," you say, "this sounds simple, but we all know it's not. So many people are out there trying so many things. What specifically should I do to grow my Social Velocity and land high-value clients?"

Fair question. To answer it, let's look again at the three specific principles you'll need in place to make sure you stand a chance of achieving your business goals.

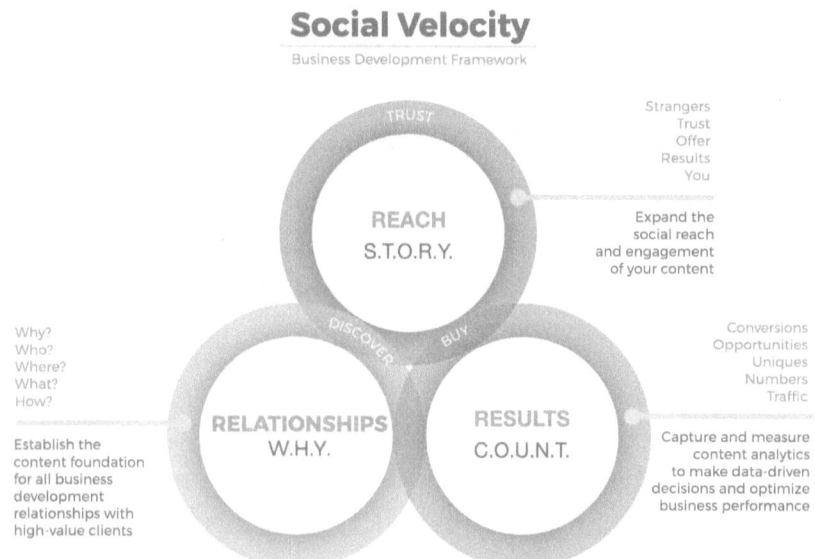

FIRST, GO WHERE YOUR CLIENTS ARE

As of this writing, LinkedIn is by far the place to be if you're interested in building quality business-to-business *relationships*, growing your social reach, and increasing your results in the slow and steady manner we've proposed in this book. Simply put, your ideal, high-value clients all have a presence on LinkedIn, so establish the right foundation and presence to meet them there. In today's social environment, it is arguable that your LinkedIn profile is more important than your website home page.

With over 740 million users, 41% of millionaires using LinkedIn for business, and 82% of all B2B leads coming from LinkedIn, you are bound to discover your sweet spot of ideal clients and build a following. And with the fact that only 1% of all LinkedIn users are consistently posting content, it would not be an understatement to say that LinkedIn is a gold mine right now. You just need the right foundation and tools to mine the gold.

SECOND, BE VISIBLE AND HELPFUL

The secret top influencers use to achieve massive **reach** on LinkedIn is to serve, not sell. If all you do is sell, you'll just be adding to the noise. But if you serve at least 80% of the time, you will earn voluntary followers in due time. And to be sure, none of this is possible if you remain the best-kept secret in your industry.

You need to be both visible and helpful, and the way to do this is to come out and tell your S.T.O.R.Y. Share thoughts, ideas, observations, and insights that will help your ideal clients improve their lives and businesses. Become a resource, a trusted advisor, and the go-to person whenever your ideal clients think of how to solve their problems. Don't worry if you're starting with an audience of just a few people. The journey of a thousand miles starts with one step. Take that first step. Get visible and helpful on LinkedIn.

THIRD, TRACK YOUR RESULTS

Once you're committed to focusing on LinkedIn to build Social Velocity, you will need to implement a proven system that measures your **results** over time. As we've discussed, if you don't measure things, you can't improve them. By building a measurable S.T.O.R.Y. funnel that tracks the results of your helpfulness and visibility, you can see what works—and what doesn't—so you can move the needle and emerge from obscurity to influence.

However, as you may have already thought, many people have tried many things with sometimes undesirable results. How will whatever system you build be any different? Again, fair question. Let's look next at some of the methods and systems others have tried so far to solve the obscurity dilemma.

23. What Others Have Tried

If you have thousands and thousands of dollars to spend on casting a wide net and testing if people will skip or block your *advertisements*, then go for it. Thousands of advertising dollars later, you will probably come to the conclusion most entrepreneurs arrive at. The return on social media ads is simply no longer what it once was.

Facebook, YouTube, Google, and other social advertising outlets have all experienced increasing costs and diminishing results over time. And LinkedIn, for all its advantages as a business-to-business hub of networking, has been well known to be the least effective and most expensive advertising platform.

To make matters worse, every prospect you get from advertising starts with a 'cold' relationship, as we've discussed in our Results Quadrant. You may have spent lots of money to get lots of Reach, but you will still need to invest more time and money to warm up the relationship sufficiently to achieve a sale. Sure, some boast about their ad strategies getting you from 'click to customer' in 24 hours, but most people who have experienced those spammy, low-integrity approaches are finally clear-eyed and ready to move on to something else that will work not only in the short run while you're paying money, but in the long run at a significantly lesser cost.

Social Velocity

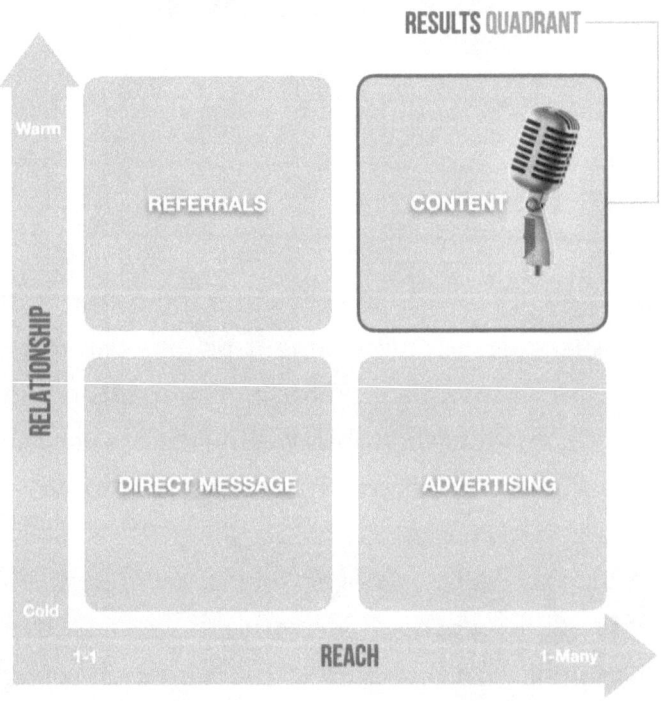

Others have also tried *direct messaging* via connection requests on LinkedIn, but the effectiveness of that strategy has been diminishing at the same rate as people are quickly recognizing it's just a ploy to try to sell you something. It's cold and has little reach unless you want to violate LinkedIn's terms of service[24] by using automation, bots, and browser plugins that could get your account banned.

And of course, there is always the idea of using manual strategies, such as *referral partnerships*, executive panels, podcast invitations, and a plethora of methods that involve one-on-one or group networking meetings to spread your message. Again, while these may be effective in building relationships, they are low in reach.

This leaves *content marketing*, which is by far the most effective, indirect method of building followership and relationships on social media. I was once surprised to hear a client tell me that she never actually realized that sharing content online could be such a powerful path to earning clients. At the same time, there are so many successful experts and influencers online today who know that their ONLY path to business success on social media has been through content marketing.

This brings us to an interesting strategy that has gained a foothold and much success for content reach all over social media, but until now, has been shrouded in confusion and never been efficiently executed.

CONTENT ENGAGEMENT

All social media platforms, such as Facebook, LinkedIn, Instagram, YouTube, etc., are content engagement systems. Heck, go ahead; call them what they really are—*Engagement Pods*. Their prime directive is simple: get people as engaged as possible for as long as possible. The more engaged 'eyeballs' they have the more premium products and advertising they can sell. Engagement is the single most important thing social platforms want from their usually 'free' user base.

However, as social media usage and traffic has grown, it has become increasingly more difficult for content creators on these platforms to get much reach, partially because the social platforms have built sophisticated algorithms to try to keep up with the traffic and automatically select what they believe are the best, most sharable posts to guarantee maximum engagement. Because of these algorithms, one can begin to see patterns of what it takes for a post to go 'viral' or be dead on arrival. Nowadays, because of increased traffic and the active selection process of algorithms, a typical post on social media gets very little traction if you have a small following.

On the positive side, these algorithms are designed to try to discover and promote quality content using a variety of criteria, such as helpfulness of content, user interactions, engagement, and compliance with the rules of their platforms.

These algorithm initiatives from social platforms have all conspired to produce a coming-together of users to try to ensure the best environment for their posts to be seen and heard. Interestingly, this has resulted in a kind of tug of war between social platforms and their users, and in the midst of it all, there is much noise and misunderstanding about what works and what doesn't, and what is ethical versus what is not.

This tug of war between social platforms and users, who ironically, both want the same thing—engagement—has a precedent in the Music and Search Engine industries. Before we dive into how content engagement works—or *should* work—let's take a look at how the need to classify, rank, and competitively prioritize information for mass consumption gave us Radio *payola* and Online S.E.O.

In the next chapter, we will describe payola and some of the ethical questions it raises. We will also discuss the global business environment that led to the rise of Google, one of the world's most powerful media companies.

24. Engagement Radio

Imagine you're driving in your car and the Deejay enthusiastically announces, "here's another one from one of the world's top, brand new artists: Ariana Grande!"

You may ask yourself, how come she's one of the world's top new artists if no one has ever heard of her before? Regardless, you listen to her song and agree; it is good. Actually, it is not just good, it is great. You smile, and you want to hear more. You may even be persuaded to buy her album. And all because you heard it on the radio!

What just happened is the core magic of radio stations. Literally out of thin air, they create the psychology of *social proof* that makes specific content 'top-of-mind' for millions of listeners. They also keep us engaged and empower the music industry that supplies them with content. Because you and I are engaged, they sell more advertising. Ariana Grande, whom no one knew last week, suddenly becomes a star, and everyone is happy.

Except, of course, the thousands of other equally talented musicians who did NOT have a record deal and were NOT therefore able to muscle their way—through *payola*—onto the radio.

The idea of 'gaming' the system to simulate social proof is legendary and has existed in multiple forms ever since the existence of mass media. Unfortunately, there is not much of an alternative for getting on the radio besides having deep pockets or a major label record deal. But here's the good news. Because of today's internet and social media, music artists can largely ignore Radio gatekeepers and independently build direct followers, a practice that has become even more powerful today than getting a record deal.

Social media is the new Radio.

Let's take a look at another example where media gatekeepers and power brokers have had to give way to more democratic systems where the power is in the hands of the people.

In the early 1990s, there were several search engines, such as AltaVista, Ask Jeeves, Excite, Infoseek, Lycos, and Yahoo. If you wanted to be discovered on any of these search engines, you had to 'rank well' by stuffing keywords into your website pages so the search engine algorithms—radio stations of a sort—could recognize your content as relevant and get you to page one of a user's search. This was the birth of search engine optimization (S.E.O.), otherwise known as a process of improving the quality and quantity of traffic to your website from organic search engine results. To ensure their SEO worked, website creators would repeat keywords hundreds of times in web page meta tags. Want to outrank someone else's page in search? Use more keywords, more times.

Naturally, the search engines didn't appreciate their systems being 'gamed' by these practices, which quickly earned the moniker '*black-hat SEO*'. In many ways, it was a user-base response to the powerful algorithms, similar in concept to how powerful Radio station Deejays would receive—from record companies—handsome payola checks to make sure they played specific artists over and over. But the key issue is that these practices are against the rules set up by all social networks, and are therefore, like payola, unethical.

In 1996, Larry Page and Sergey Brin, two Stanford University students, began their search engine, which would eventually become what we know today as Google. They approached the need to get to page one from a different, more user-driven perspective. Their original algorithm—known as PageRank—allowed the collective user base to *organically* decide what gets seen on page one of a search result, versus relying on individual website powerbrokers or keyword stuffers alone. Their idea was simple, rank and order search results on the web by link popularity. A page would therefore rank higher if it had more qualified links pointing to it. Now, if you wanted to get seen on page one of a search engine, then many *other* users had to show that they had *engaged* with your page by linking to it, as opposed to you independently stuffing your page with keywords.

This new approach to being 'discovered' by a search engine was revolutionary! Before Google's PageRank algorithm, search engines ranked sites primarily based on whatever keywords were found 'on-page' within a site's pages. Google's approach changed the game by looking at both on-page and off-page factors, such as how many other quality websites pointed links to your content.

Google's algorithm turned the paradigms of radio station payola and black-hat SEO inside out. In essence, Google was saying:

"If lots of people are linking to you, they are talking about you, and if they are talking about you, you must be worthy of being seen by more people."

They were using whatever social proof existed to rank content, as opposed to creating the illusion of popularity from thin air as the radio stations did. In the old model, if you heard Ariana Grande on the radio, the perception was that millions of other people were hearing it as well, the psychology of social proof would kick in, and you were sold! In Google's model, the *listeners* would have to all call in to a radio station voluntarily to report how much they loved a specific artist. Google's social proof approach went on to dominate the industry and the rest is history.

Now let's turn our attention back to social media and content marketing. Google's social proof approach carried over to social media platforms as algorithms were increasingly set up to try to bring the 'best' user content into their feeds based on how others were engaging with it.

Naturally, you can imagine that very soon, the user base on social media started to discover ways of providing whatever the algorithms needed to push content as far as possible. As you might imagine, this meant that some methods were—again—not entirely ethical. History began to repeat itself. In the days of Radio, we saw payola. In the early days of search engines, we saw keyword stuffing and black-hat SEO. Now, in the world of social media, we have what I call speed-based, hustle-focused, *black-hat content engagement*. It's all human nature. Not much has changed.

But there is a better, more ethical way.

In the SEO world, there is something called 'white-hat S.E.O.', which as you can imagine, is the positive opposite of black-hat SEO. White-hat SEO is when website owners use SEO strategies and tactics that *comply* with the terms and conditions of search engines. Not only were these strategies ethical, but they were also safer and worked better.

This approach was what set up our main inspiration for what I now call *White-hat C.E.O. (content engagement optimization)*. By definition, this is when users deploy content engagement strategies that are in line with the spirit, terms, and conditions of a social platform. Let's take a look at how and why white-hat C.E.O. is the key to getting high-value clients online.

25. White-Hat C.E.O.

As we've seen from our brief histories of the music and search engine industries, social proof is a key element in any decision about whether content will be viewed by observers or the powers that be as important, high-quality, or not. In Radio, we saw that the perception of quality was easily manufactured for listeners through Deejay payola. In search engines, we saw that black-hat SEO methods could 'game' the algorithms to create temporary gains in search engine results. We then saw how Google introduced the idea of social proof to the equation. Finally, we saw how white-hat SEO emerged as a compliant, ethical approach to improving page rank results.

We've also seen similarities between the social media and search engine landscapes. Like the Google algorithm, the LinkedIn algorithm responds to whatever social proof shows up on a post in the form of 'views', 'likes', 'comments', shares, and so on. In essence, whatever content gets high user *engagement* is seen by LinkedIn as being 'on the radio', and therefore it gets promoted even further.

Social Velocity

 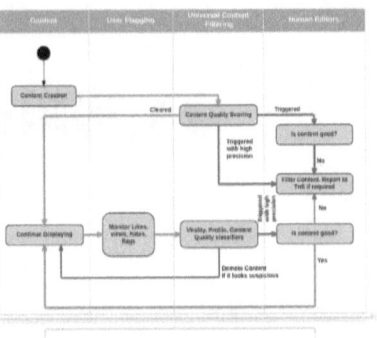

As in the search engine industry, social media users have a choice. When trying to increase the engagement, ranking, and reach of a post, they can either go black-hat or focus on integrity, with white-hat CEO. Let's take a look at some of the differences in approach between these two choices:

	Black-Hat Engagement	White-Hat Engagement
Terms of Service	Doing things in violation of TOS	Always being in compliance with TOS
Algorithm	Instant gratification to 'game' the algorithm	Delayed gratification to 'ride' the algorithm
Humans or Bots	Automations, bots, browser plugins engaging on your behalf	No bots, ever. Real human beings interacting with real human beings
Content Quality	Low quality content	High quality content that produces reach
Engagement	Fake engagement that produces only vanity metrics	Real engagement that creates clients
Paradigm	Speed	Social Velocity

I was honored to be joined on The Profitable Happiness Podcast[25] by Rand Fishkin, one of the pioneers of white-hat SEO. As founder of the leading SEO firm, MOZ, and one of the most highly respected individuals in SEO, Rand explained to me his firm's singular focus on *integrity*. Here are his own words about the founding of MOZ:

"From the very beginning, we felt passionate about bringing integrity to the frustratingly opaque SEO industry." - Rand Fishkin

In the middle of this choice between black-hat and white-hat methods, there is a lot of online misinformation. When some people hear the word 'engagement' they think it's all bad because of the bad press that black-hat engagement has created. The truth is, there is a way to do engagement ethically, and that's what white-hat engagement is all about.

Before we dive into exactly how white-hat CEO works, let's take a quick look at engagement pods, the user-driven phenomenon that has risen to address the need for increased content engagement on social media.

ENGAGEMENT PODS

An engagement pod is simply a group of people coming together in agreement to engage with each other's posts. On the surface, this is perfectly within the rules of social platforms, except when you look deeper and discover that certain groups are using bots, automation, plugins, and various inauthentic methods to try to 'game' the algorithms. (Sound familiar?) It's worth repeating here that any attempt to violate a social network's rules and regulations is not acceptable and should not be tolerated.

Most engagement pods that are playing fair and within the rules use a variety of inefficient methods provided by social networks to notify people within their group about posts so that they can join in the conversation. One thing a lot of people do not realize is how prevalent engagement strategies are within social media. When a company employee posts an article on LinkedIn and emails everyone on their team to jump into the discussion, that's an engagement pod. Whenever you use hashtags or tags or groups to increase the number of eyeballs and engagement on your new post, that's an engagement pod. For all the negative press about engagement pods online, they are a rather pervasive and normal part of social media ecosystems. Social media platforms want as much engagement as possible.

Here is a non-comprehensive list of strategies that people and companies have tried for increasing engagement on their content:

1. Embedding hashtags in a post to broadcast it to others on the social platform.
2. Tagging individual people on a social platform to get their attention so they can come and engage with a specific post.

3. Direct messaging within a social platform or sending email to specific people who agree to engage with each other's posts.
4. Joining a WhatsApp, Facebook, LinkedIn, or other group to discover when a post has been sent out by one of the members.

There are certainly other strategies out there, but they mostly struggle either because of inefficiency or because they are black-hat. Here are some of the challenges they all face:

- People who join these groups are bombarded with content, most of which is uninteresting and irrelevant to them. Trying to engage with so much incoming content quickly becomes overwhelming and leads to burnout.
- Some engagement groups *require* engagement, which makes the above-mentioned overwhelm even worse.
- These groups are highly disorganized and inefficient for meeting some of the requirements of the social algorithms, such as how many people engage within a specific time. If people show up whenever they want, there is a fair chance that you may get some interaction, but it won't affect your post's chances of being seen.
- There is a general lack of quality monitoring, which results in inauthentic content from people whose only purpose is to get reach and have no interest in meaningful conversations.
- Most of the manual approaches are inefficient, and the automated ones are black-hat because of their use of bots posting and commenting in your name. As we've made very

clear, we strongly suggest staying away from automated engagement pod systems.
- None of these approaches help you build better relationships through your content. They don't tell you what's working or not working with your content, so you're essentially chasing vanity metrics such as likes and views. Your content is not leading to any improvement in messaging, targeting, or business development.

Despite all the challenges and bad press about engagement pods, one thing is true across the board.

No matter how inefficient, they work!

Many of today's top social media influencers have shared, albeit privately or within their closed networks, that they would not be where they are today had it not been for engagement pods early in their careers.

So, the question one has to consider is this: is there a way to get engagement on content to expand reach, relationships, and results, while doing so *ethically* and within the rules of social media platforms?

The answer is enthusiastically, YES, and the best evidence I've seen is from LinkedIn themselves in their product: LinkedIn Elevate.

LINKEDIN ELEVATE

Many of today's companies have come to realize that their employees can speak with a more authentic voice than the parent brand. As such, they increasingly rely on their employees to grow their brands on social media. To support and encourage the sharing of company information on social media, they install 'employee advocacy' programs to help increase the organic reach and engagement of their content. In short, they promote their organizations through their workforce.

Naturally, LinkedIn saw the employee advocacy niche as a profit center and developed LinkedIn Elevate, which they describe thus:

*LinkedIn Elevate is a new product that helps companies and employees **curate** high-quality content, **share** easily to social networks, and **measure** the impact[26].*

The real power of LinkedIn Elevate was its ability to provide features that kept company-related social sharing top-of-mind for employees so that collectively, they would increase the reach and engagement on all content from the parent brand.

In short, LinkedIn Elevate was white-hat CEO.

I describe it in the past tense because, as of 2020, LinkedIn made the decision to merge the features of Elevate with their Company Pages features[27]. In essence, they've made their content engagement tools freely available within the platform for companies to leverage.

If there was ever any evidence that white-hat CEO was possible, this was it. LinkedIn Elevate proved that engagement and social reach was possible with the right tools.

LinkedIn Elevate, albeit targeted at companies, quickly became one of our greatest sources of inspiration in developing ClientJam for entrepreneurs and small businesses. We wanted to build a system that efficiently helps you use content marketing to get high-value clients (not just engagement for vanity metrics). We also wanted to build a system that played 100% within the rules of social networks. After much research and development, we came up with ClientJam, the world's first white-hat C.E.O. (content engagement optimization) system that increases the relationships, reach, and results of your content so that you can land your highest-value clients on social media.

Ready to see how it works? Awesome!

It's time to Jam!

26. ClientJam

ClientJam is both a software capability and a community that combines three important elements for landing high-value clients online:

1. A community of practice and a quality feedback system where people help each other build *relationships* with high-value clients and grow their businesses through content marketing.
2. A white-hat C.E.O. (content engagement optimization) tool that plays 100% by the rules of social media platforms to ethically expand content *reach*.
3. An analytics environment that shows you exactly what is working (and what's not working) in your *results* so you can measure—and therefore improve—your content marketing over time.

When we first launched ClientJam, we received some excellent testimonials, a few of which I'd like to share with you before I explain exactly how it works:

"Happy Friday, Dr. Pelè! I just wanted to reach out to you and thank you for putting ClientJam together. Yesterday was my first Jam. To be honest, I'm an old-fashioned face-to-face marketing person. I've always struggled with converting to the new social media age of marketing because it felt so superficial to me. I just started investing in my professional online presence about a year and a half ago.

I've recently changed my business model from being just a writer with gigs to becoming a business owner, and it's been a learning curve for me. I can't believe that I put my head in the sand instead of just diving in. ClientJam is unbelievable. It feels like I'm in a club with members who are working together to help each other.

It feels like networking without the pressure of trying to land clients even though you know you are increasing engagement to increase visibility to attract potential clients. I've always felt like I had to force myself to engage on LinkedIn because there are too many platforms to keep up with, but using ClientJam feels like an organic process for me because I can engage with people I find interesting and have intentional conversations sparked by mutual interest." - Ally

Here's another one:

"I love that ClientJam is filled with a supportive community of professionals who are invested in each other's success. The tool itself makes it easy to get more engagement and exposure on LinkedIn, and the community makes that engagement meaningful. No bots here!" - Heather

And another one:

"ClientJam increased my content popularity by 729.93% in my first month!" - Jim

And another one:

"ClientJam is helping me with consistency!" - Kym

And another one:

"ClientJam is a game-changer for my business!" - Cheryl

All of these testimonials were possible because we have very carefully crafted a white-hat CEO content engagement system that delivers results. Let's look at the main features of ClientJam by starting with a few of the things we believe are important for you to launch a successful content marketing strategy:

- Consistency
- Content
- Connections
- Conversations
- Community

Consistency

The key to growing your authority through social media is consistency. When you post helpful content on a scheduled, regular, ongoing basis, you earn trust from your target audience, which over time, will translate into higher interest for your services. I call this the 'Oprah Effect'. Every evening, at 4pm when Oprah was on her network, everyone wanted to see that show and they knew it was always going to be there at 4pm. And because of that consistency, she was able to grow a large audience. By encouraging and implementing consistency, you turn your content marketing into a legitimate, organic lead generation source.

Content

The quality and helpfulness of your content are directly related to whether your ideal clients will take steps to learn more about you or not. The key is therefore to make sure you produce high-quality, conversion-focused content that reaches the right people. Vanity metrics—such as post views—are irrelevant if no one takes action on your content. By the way, when we say high quality, we're not talking about the quality of the production. We are talking about the quality of the content and the message itself. Your goal is to create high-quality content that has Social Velocity so that it reaches more of your ideal clients and *moves* them to take action with you.

Connection

The purpose of your content is to create an emotional, logical, and instinctual reaction from your intended audience so that they can begin to move toward you over time. Every post is a chance to exchange value and touch people on these multiple cerebral levels from which all decisions emanate. The more you connect, the more engaged your audience will be.

Conversations

The purpose of content marketing is to inspire *conversations that create clients*. It's through ongoing engagement and dialog over time that the best business relationships are built. Don't ask for marriage on a first date! Produce content that drives conversations, and from there, builds trust and converts prospects into clients.

Community

A vibrant community of practice is essential if you want to truly improve your content in the market. With a good community, you'll get feedback, recognition, a chance to practice, and perhaps even emotional rewards when people who share a common goal interact with your content. As the African proverb goes, "if you want to go fast, go alone. But if you want to go far, go together."

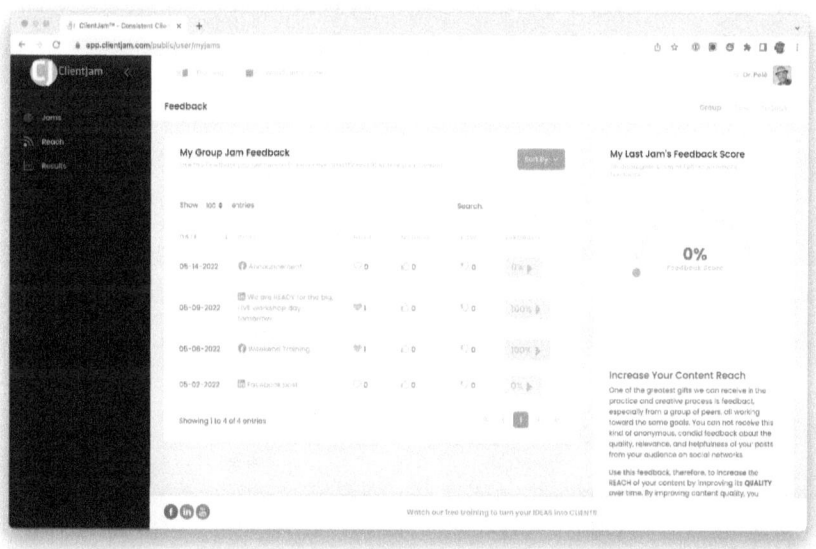

IT'S TIME TO JAM

When you think of the word 'Jam', do you think of a traffic jam, or do you think of the kind of jam that might go on bread? Or do you think of a Jam as when musicians come together? Well, the last example is what inspired the name 'ClientJam'. A 'Jam' is when musicians improvise and spontaneously create beauty. Sometimes a Jam is solo, when a musician just wants to 'jam' along to a pre-recorded track. Sometimes a Jam is when people come together in groups to create that beauty together. Regardless of how it happens, the intention is always the same; a free flowing of ideas, instant feedback, fun, mastery, and a sense of both personal and community mission.

Lately, the idea of something being 'your Jam' has come to mean something special outside of music. While 'your Jam' used to refer to your favorite song, nowadays, it can refer to anything special and favored by you.

These are the inspirational hooks behind the idea of a Jam in the name 'ClientJam', the software and community where Social Velocity goes to *thrive*.

ClientJam is our hub for building Social Velocity through Relationships, Reach, and Results from content marketing. It is where our community of coaches, consultants, entrepreneurs, and companies come together to individually and collectively improve their content marketing results and land high-value clients.

HOW CLIENTJAM WORKS

As we've mentioned, ClientJam is an organized, efficient way of ethically implementing your content marketing strategy on LinkedIn. With all the approaches so far discussed, we believe ClientJam offers a comprehensive toolkit to help execute a successful content marketing strategy on social media. Here is a non-comprehensive view of some ClientJam features.

Dr. Pelè

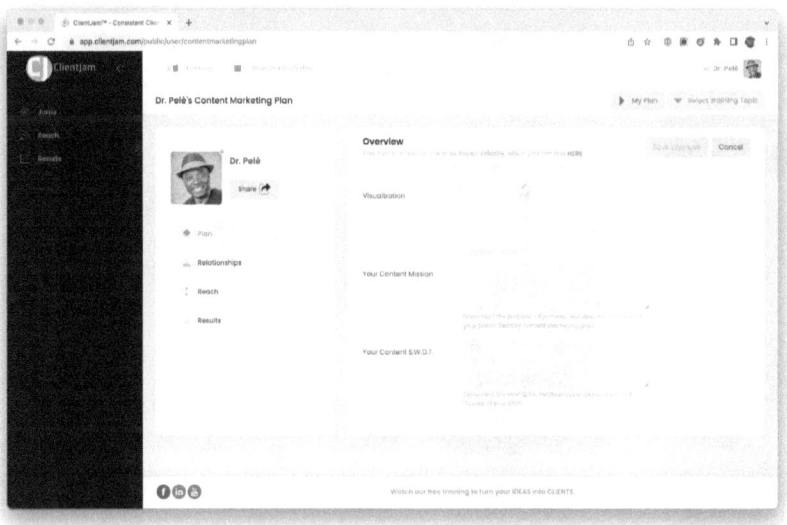

1. *Your Content Marketing Plan*

It all starts with the idea that you need a plan if you're going to be successful. As such, we provide you a place to record your content marketing plan according to the elements we've described in this book. You can also print and export your plan and share or discuss it with your team or colleagues.

This is a limited, free section of ClientJam, which you can access as a gift for reading this book. Just visit Clientjam.com and create your free account! You can get a lot of mileage just by investing the time to actually create a content marketing plan.

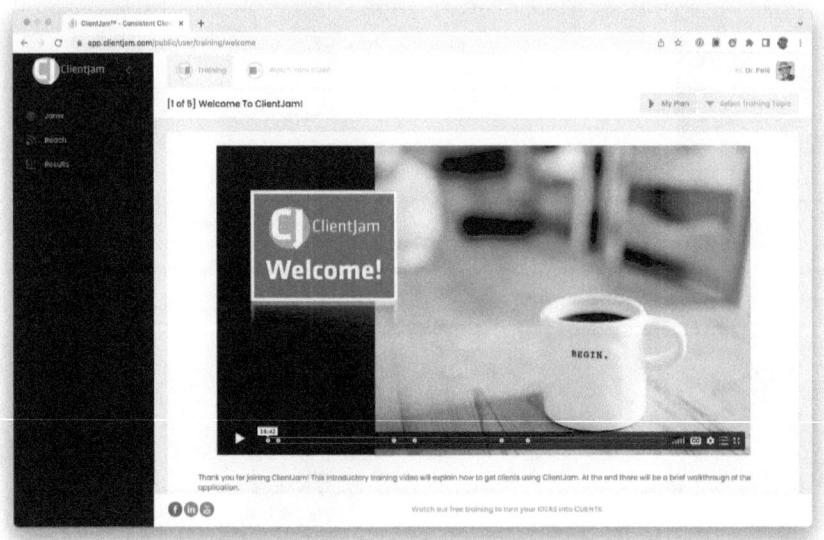

2. *Comprehensive Training*

Before you can fully use ClientJam, we take you through a short, but comprehensive training program that will teach you the details of how to craft excellent content that will land you high-value clients.

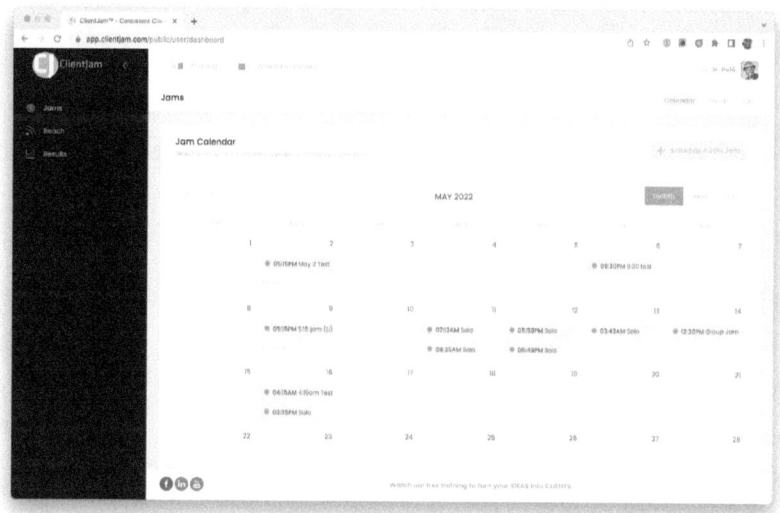

3. *Your Jams*

Once you complete the training and gain access to the full features of ClientJam, you'll begin with the concept of a 'Jam', which is when you show up on a calendar either by yourself (solo), or join a group of others (group) to post your content on LinkedIn (or other platforms) at a scheduled time.

The first step is to select either a solo Jam—when you want to jam by yourself—or join a group Jam at a specific time determined by the system. This calendar alone has resulted in huge efficiencies on the group side because reminders and other systems ensure that everyone shows up on time and participates as promised, which is a huge improvement to several of the manual engagement approaches we've discussed already.

4. Content Planning and Ideas

Next up is the I.D.E.A.S. 365 calendar, where you plan and schedule your content and also download free content posting templates for every day of the year. If you download our templates, use them only as a starting point. Your final content would come from performing keyword searches on Google to discover what topics are trending and are in demand by your ideal clients. One easy way to do this is to simply type in a search term on Google, and then see what other suggested topics show up in the search bar. Those topics are actually what other people interested in your keyword have *already* been searching for. This is a powerful way to make sure that your content is relevant and timely for your ideal clients. With this kind of firepower, it would be difficult to ever run out of ideas for executing your content marketing plan.

5. It's Jam Time!

Next, you have the Jam itself, as well as the opportunity for community feedback so you can get better with your content marketing.

Every Jam is organized for maximum engagement and according to the white-hat CEO approaches we've described previously. There are absolutely zero database connections or software interactions between ClientJam and any social network. The tool is 100% compliant with all of their rules and regulations. Whether you're in a solo Jam or a group Jam, you have the opportunity to post your content, invite others to voluntarily engage with your content, and get their feedback—anonymously—so you can learn what's working and what can be improved with your content over time.

6. Your Results

And finally, there is the results section, where you get interactive graphs, gamification, charts, and tables that show you analytics covering how people are interacting with your content so you can optimize your marketing over time. This is truly the heart of white-hat content engagement optimization (CEO). Like the Waggle dance of the honeybee, this is where your content shows you what's working or not.

Whether you do a solo Jam or a group Jam, the key is that you need analytics to tell you what's working or what's not. It would take hours of scrolling on a social media network, and documentation on spreadsheets to try to get the kind of information you need to make good content marketing decisions. With ClientJam, it's all available to you instantly and in one place so you can measure your progress over time.

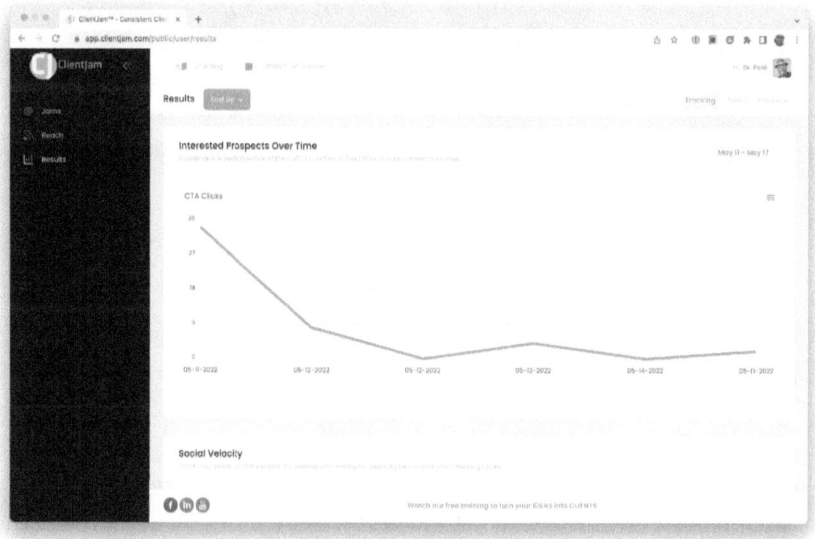

LET'S RECAP

Your goal as a coach, consultant, entrepreneur, or company can be described in one sentence:

Get High-Value Clients With Content Marketing!

We've discussed the fact that anyone who begins a content marketing journey will likely face three challenges:

1. **How do you get high-value clients through content marketing?** It's not enough to connect with people on social media. You will need a plan, implementation tools, and a community so you can attract followers and build authentic business *relationships*.
2. **How do you stand out from the crowd?** No matter how excellent your product, it is of no use if no one ever sees you. You will need to increase the *reach* of your content so that you are visible to more of your ideal clients.
3. **How do you know what's working (or not)?** You can't improve what you can't measure. You need detailed *analytics* for your profile and content so you can improve your **results** over time.

We've also talked about the fact that with only 1% of LinkedIn's 740 million + users posting consistently, now is a great time and a huge opportunity to become an effective content creator on the platform.

We've shared the clear choice we've made toward integrity by moving *away* from 'speedy', 'hamster wheel', 'hustling', and 'black-hat' engagement methods. Our unique, ethical approach through 'white-hat CEO' will allow you to 'ride' the algorithms to success in compliance, not 'game' them. We help you stick 100% within the rules and regulations of social platforms.

ClientJam's tools and training will empower you to use your content to build ***Social Velocity*** through better business relationships, reach, and results.

RELATIONSHIPS: Build powerful **relationships** on by consistently posting helpful content that speaks directly to the needs of your ideal clients.

REACH: Expand the **reach** of your social content posts by attracting high-quality, inbound engagement from your target audience.

RESULTS: Make the **results** of your content visible so you can see what works (or what doesn't) as you improve your process of attracting your ideal clients.

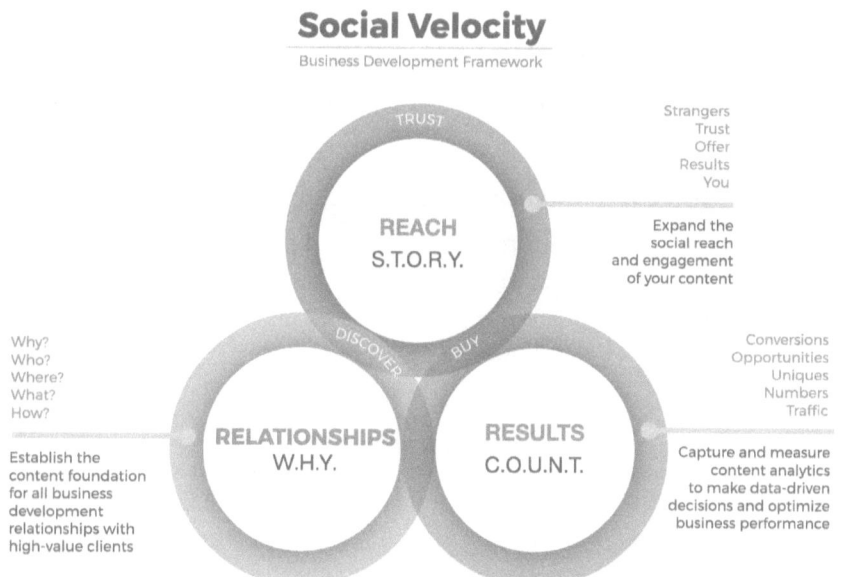

So, let's circle back to where we started. Is marketing dead? I suppose that's debatable. However, what is not controversial is that companies and entrepreneurs alike can now leverage social media to significantly increase business success. If you are a consultant, coach, or company, now is the time to begin sharing helpful content that builds *relationships*, *reach*, and *results*, for that is truly the path to creating long-term business success.

Once there was Interruption Marketing. Then there was Permission Marketing. My hope is that now, there is *Social Velocity*.

If you've enjoyed this book and decide to go on and implement content marketing as we've described it, you will be joining us to usher in an age of great storytelling, helpfulness, and Social Velocity.

Are you ready? Are you ready to shift from speed to velocity? From going fast to going far? Are you fired up and ready to begin a content marketing journey to land your highest-value clients?

If so, join us by starting with a free account on ClientJam. Once there, create your plan and get ready for content marketing success. And if that's a good start for you, consider getting 1-1 mentorship for help launching a successful content marketing strategy for your business.

Thank you for taking the time to read this book. I look forward to meeting you in our community and to being of service in any way that I can. I wish you love, peace, and profitable happiness.

Let's Jam!

DR. PELÈ

Dr. Pelè is a bestselling author, musician, educator, and founder of ClientJam, where he partners with professionals to build Social Velocity, which turns their authentic content into clients.

Born in a war-torn African village, he has experienced both humble beginnings and the victory of the American dream. His unique journey has taught him what truly drives success—and it's not who or what we are. It's how well we leverage happiness and harmony—the music of our lives.

Dr. Pelè holds a Ph.D. in Organization and Management. He has delivered global learning solutions to Fortune 500 clients, won numerous speaking awards, and landed songs on top Billboard and UK music charts.

Today, Dr. Pelè artfully combines his passions for music and education to help people close the gap between potential and performance.

Contact Dr. Pelè at **www.drpele.com**

REFERENCES

Chapter 1

1. "What Is Marketing? - The Definition of Marketing - AMA." *American Marketing Association*, www.ama.org/the-definition-of-marketing-what-is-marketing/.
2. "185: The Practice Of Shipping Creativity, With Seth Godin." Dr. Pelè, drpele.com/185-the-practice-of-shipping-creativity-with-seth-godin/.
3. PK;, Mischel W;Shoda Y;Peake. "The Nature of Adolescent Competencies Predicted by Preschool Delay of Gratification." Journal of Personality and Social Psychology, U.S. National Library of Medicine, pubmed.ncbi.nlm.nih.gov/3367285/.
4. RN;, Kidd C;Palmeri H;Aslin. "Rational Snacking: Young Children's Decision-Making on the Marshmallow Task Is Moderated by Beliefs about Environmental Reliability." Cognition, U.S. National Library of Medicine, pubmed.ncbi.nlm.nih.gov/23063236/.
5. Bird, Alexander. "Thomas Kuhn." Stanford Encyclopedia of Philosophy, Stanford University, 31 Oct. 2018, plato.stanford.edu/entries/thomas-kuhn/.

Chapter 2

6. Ugboajah, Dr. Pelè Raymond. Narrative as Influence: A Delphi Study of Storytelling as an Entrepreneurial Leadership Best Practice, Capella University, ProQuest Dissertations Publishing, 2007, https://search.proquest.com/openview/7b7f6a07e5f9e4b2948418c121e79253/1.pdf?pq-origsite=gscholar&cbl=18750&diss=y
7. Google Trends, Google, trends.google.com/trends.
8. "Poor Richard's Almanack." Benjamin Franklin Historical Society, www.benjamin-franklin-history.org/poor-richards-almanac/.
9. "The Works of Benjamin Franklin, Vol. I Autobiography, Letters and Misc. Writings 1725-1734." Online Library of Liberty, oll.libertyfund.org/title/bigelow-the-works-of-benjamin-franklin-vol-i-autobiography-letters-and-misc-writings-1725-1734.
10. Ugboajah, Dr. Pelè Raymond. Big-Ticket Clients: You Can't Catch A Whale With A Worm™ (How To Use The Psychology Of Story To Land Big-Ticket Clients Online, While Being Your Most Authentic Self): Raymond Ugboajah, Dr. Pelè: 9781096342298: Amazon.com: Books, amzn.to/3kTJwre.
11. "Alexander O'Neal: Lovers Again." Billboard, Hot 100, https://www.billboard.com/music/alexander-oneal/chart-history/hot-adult-r-and-b-airplay/song/58057.
12. Holmes, Chet. "The Ultimate Sales Machine." NEW Chapter 4, chetholmes.com/wp-content/uploads/2018/01/NEW-Chapter-4-1-1.pdf.

Chapter 4

13. LinkedIn Newsroom. "About LinkedIn." LinkedIn Newsroom, news.linkedin.com/about-us#Statistics.
14. 11th Annual "B2B Content Marketing 2021 - Benchmarks, Budgets and Trends ." https://contentmarketinginstitute.com/wp-content/uploads/2020/09/b2b-2021-research-final.pdf

Chapter 10

15. Cialdini, R. B. (2001). Influence: Science and practice (4th ed.). Boston: Allyn & Bacon. ISBN 978-0-205-60999-4.

Chapter 11

16. "2016 Content Preferences Survey: B2B Buyers Value Content That Offers Data And Analysis." Demand Gen Report, www.demandgenreport.com/resources/research/2016-content-preferences-survey-b2b-buyers-value-content-that-offers-data-and-analysis.

Chapter 12

17. "Strategies for Keeping the LinkedIn Feed Relevant." LinkedIn Engineering, engineering.linkedin.com/blog/2017/03/strategies-for-keeping-the-linkedin-feed-relevant.

Chapter 13

18. "182: Relentlessly Helpful Content DNA, With John Espirian." *Dr. Pelè*, drpele.com/182-relentlessly-helpful-content-dna-with-john-espirian/.
19. "148: Neil Patel's Digital Marketing Success Strategy." *Dr. Pelè*, drpele.com/neil-patels-digital-marketing-success-strategy/.

Chapter 14

20. CBS News. (2011, October 23). *60 Minutes* full coverage: Steve Jobs. Retrieved from https://www.cbsnews.com/news/60-minutes-full-coverage-steve-jobs/

Chapter 15

21. Nielsen. (2012). Global Trust in Advertising and Brand Messages. Retrieved from https://www.nielsen.com/content/dam/corporate/us/en/reports-downloads/2012-Reports/global-trust-in-advertising-2012.pdf
22. Jantsch, J. (2013). *The Referral Engine: Teaching Your Business How to Market Itself*. London: Portfolio.

Chapter 22

23. Staff, Chief Marketer. "Consumers Are Marketing Saturated: Yankelovich." *Chief Marketer*, Chief Marketer, 30 Nov. -1, www.chiefmarketer.com/consumers-are-marketing-saturated-yankelovich/.

Chapter 23

24. "User Agreement ." *LinkedIn*, www.linkedin.com/legal/user-agreement#dos

Chapter 25

25. "062: Transparency And Painful Honesty For Startups With Rand Fishkin." *Dr. Pelè*, drpele.com/062-transparency-and-painful-honesty-for-startups-with-rand-fishkin/.
26. Sun, Will. "Introducing LinkedIn Elevate: Helping Companies Empower Their Employees To Share Content." *Recent Posts*, 2015, blog.linkedin.com/2015/04/13/elevate.
27. Jobanputra, Rishi. "LinkedIn Pages and Elevate - Better Together." *LinkedIn Marketing Blog*, 2020, business.linkedin.com/marketing-solutions/blog/linkedin-company-pages/2020/linkedin-pages-and-elevate--better-together.

www.ingramcontent.com/pod-product-compliance
Lightning Source LLC
Chambersburg PA
CBHW020640220526
45464CB00001B/223